STECK-VAUGHN

DEVELOPING
READING
Strategies

EDITORIAL CONSULTANTS

Mary Sue Dillingofski, Ph.D.
Reading Specialist
Educational Consultant
Chicago, Illinois

James P. Menconi
Reading Specialist
Chicago Public Schools
Chicago, Illinois

Betty Willis, Ph.D.
K-12 Reading Specialist
Cypress - Fairbanks School District
Houston, Texas

Challenges

Project Design and Development: E.L. Wheetley & Associates, Inc.
Cover Design and Development: D. Childress
Cover Photography: © Keith Gunnar/FPG

**DEVELOPING READING STRATEGIES is a series of six
titles listed in recommended sequence:**

> **CHALLENGES**
> **Quests**
> **Ventures**
> **Insights**
> **Summits**
> **Horizons**

Published by

STECK-VAUGHN
C O M P A N Y
A Subsidiary of National Education Corporation

Printed in the United States of America.

ISBN 0-8114-5850-4

7 8 9 10 C 99 98 97 96

CONTENTS

Survival

Read and learn about survival

Most of us think our lives are dull sometimes. We often do the same things every day. Still, we dream about excitement. We long for new challenges. We think of ourselves in life-and-death struggles—that we always win, of course.

For some people, the dreams become true. Without warning, normal life stops. Danger is on all sides. These people often find that the dreams are really nightmares. To win a life-and-death struggle is not easy. Yet many people do win such struggles. They survive. And they are not disabled by their struggles for survival. Instead, they become stronger.

What do you already know about survival?

Talk about what you know. Get together with a group of students to talk about what you already know about survival. Here are some questions to help you get started.
1. How could you prepare for boating in waters where man-eating sharks swim?
2. How can you keep yourself and others calm in danger?
3. How would you keep warm if you were alone in ice and snow for a long time?

Write about what you know. Choose a life-or-death situation such as being caught in a burning building or being on a sinking ship. Write what you could do to survive.

_____

_____

_____

Make predictions

Read the titles of the articles in this cluster and look at the picture of the shark on page 5. Write down three things you expect to learn by reading these articles.

1. _____

2. _____

3. _____

Start to learn new word meanings

The words listed below are used in the two paragraphs at the top of page 4. Study the meanings of these words as you read about survival.

challenge—something that needs skills and hard work. *The biggest challenge was surviving the cold nights.*

disabled—not able to perform in the usual way. *Sharks circled the boat after it was disabled by the storm.*

Learn new skills and strategies

In this cluster you will learn about finding the main idea in a paragraph. Finding the main idea as you are reading helps you keep track of the most important information. Other skills you will learn about are making predictions and using a dictionary.

Gather new information

By the end of this cluster, you will have learned some answers to these questions.

1. What can people learn at wilderness schools?
2. How are swimmers affected by ocean currents?
3. How can you use your head when your life is in danger?
4. Who was one of the bravest explorers of Antarctica?
5. What are some dangers of flying in a hot-air balloon?

Outward Bound

What do you already know?
Write down three facts that you already know about camping, hiking, or surviving in the wilderness. Work with a partner, if you like.

1. _____

2. _____

3. _____

Make predictions
Look at the pictures and headings, or words in large type, in the article. Then write down three things that you think you will learn as you read this article.

1. _____

2. _____

3. _____

Set your purpose for reading
Write down one thing you hope to find out about surviving in the mountains or Outward Bound as you read this article.

_____

_____

_____

Learn important words
Study the meanings of the words below and how they are used in sentences. Knowing these words might help you as you read this article.

challenge—something that needs skills and hard work. *Climbing up the side of the mountain was a big challenge.*

disabled—not able to perform in the usual way. *The disabled boy got over the wall, even though he was in a wheelchair.*

mountaineering—the sport of mountain climbing. *Mountaineering is a hard sport to learn.*

Are you 14 or older? If you are, you can learn survival skills in Outward Bound classes. You can go to the Rocky Mountains to learn mountaineering. You can learn white-water rafting on a river. Outward Bound classes are hard. How much you learn depends on the kind of challenge you want.

Disabled students take part in Outward Bound classes. In one class, students went to a 14-foot-high wooden wall. The instructor said, "Everybody over the wall!" The students thought. Then they climbed on one another's shoulders. All made it over—except the last boy. He was in a wheelchair. Soon the students found a way to hang the next-to-last boy over the wall by his ankles. He reached the wrists of the last boy. Then everyone pulled him and his wheelchair over!

Using skills and strategies

Main idea

Imagine that you went to an Outward Bound class. You come home and tell friends what you did in your classes. You tell them about one thing you did, and then you tell them about something else. Writers do the same thing; they write about one topic at a time. Writers put all the sentences about a topic in a paragraph. When they write about a new topic, they put the sentences about that topic in a new paragraph.

The topic of a paragraph—what it's about—is called its *main idea*. Read the first two paragraphs again. Can you figure out their main ideas? The main ideas are underlined for you.

In Outward Bound classes, students hike in the mountains and develop survival skills.

7

<u>The disabled boy helped another student the next day.</u>
One of the others in this class began to panic during a
canoe-overturning drill. The handicapped boy was a strong
swimmer. He kept the other boy steady through the drill.

Students at Outward Bound learn by facing challenges.
The mountaineering class begins with a one-mile run up a
steep mountain road. Students wonder, "What did I get
myself into?" During the three-week course, the class learns
to read maps. They study first aid. They climb mountain
peaks. For three days, each student camps alone. On the
last day, everyone runs ten miles in the mountains.

Using skills and strategies

Main idea

The first paragraph on this page tells how the disabled
boy helped another student. The sentence in the paragraph
that states this main idea is underlined.

Here are the main ideas of the four paragraphs below.

A. A girl learns the first step in mountaineering.
B. A girl tells what she gained from Outward Bound.
C. After problems, the girl gives up on her climb.
D. A girl succeeds and feels great about it.

Read each paragraph. Decide which paragraph tells about
each idea. Then write the letter of the main idea at the left
of its paragraph.

During one mountaineering class, a young girl tried to
grab part of the steep, smooth rock. The soles of her shoes
kept sliding back to the ground. Finally she figured out how
to anchor her feet. She climbed up the steep rock. She was
mountaineering! The young girl was doing something she
never thought she could do.

The next climb was harder. The girl reached for a hand-
hold that was too high. She began slipping. The girl kept
searching for a place to hold on. She bruised her arms and
legs on the rock. After trying for a long time, she asked to
get down. She said, "I felt as if I had failed. Worst of all, I
failed in front of all the other students."

Her knees shaking, the girl tried again. She tied herself
onto the rope and began climbing. This time she reached
the top. Later, she explained how she felt. "Making it to the
top of that climb was one of the best moments of my life. I
thought I had let the other students down. But all they
cared about was that I was really trying."

"For the rest of the course I faced bigger challenges. I
knew that if I had done what I had done the day before,
then I could face this new challenge now. When the course
was over, I went home. Now I face different challenges. I tell
myself that if I could do the things I did at Outward Bound,
I can do what I need to do now."

Think About What You've Read

Important ideas

1. Name a course Outward Bound offers.

_____

2. How can facing challenges at Outward Bound help students at home?

_____

_____

Use what you've learned before

3. The article told about some of the things that students do at Outward Bound. What other things do you think the students do?

_____

_____

Important word meanings

Circle the words _challenge_ and _mountaineering_ in the article. Then pretend you are taking a mountaineering class. Write what you think would be the biggest challenge for you in the class.

_____

_____

Using skills and strategies

Look back at the article. What is the main idea of the second paragraph on page 8? Underline the first sentence. That sentence tells the main idea.

Writing

Write a newspaper ad for Outward Bound schools. Tell about the classes offered. Use your own paper or a poster.

Your important ideas

Look back over the article. Write down one idea that seems to be the most important one to you.

_____

Your important words

Look back at the words you have learned as you read about Outward Bound. Write down the word or words that you think are most important.

_____

Alone in the Ocean

What do you already know?

Write three facts that you think you already know about the ocean. You might write about plant and animal life in the ocean, survival in the water, or boating in the ocean. Work with a partner, if you like.

1. _____

2. _____

3. _____

Make predictions

Look at the pictures and the first paragraph of the article. Then write down three facts you think you will learn as you read this article.

1. _____

2. _____

3. _____

Set your purpose for reading

Write down one thing that you hope to find out about the ocean—or survival in the ocean—as you read this article.

_____

_____

_____

Learn important words

Study the meanings of the words below and how they are used in sentences. Knowing these words might help you as you read this article.

coast—land along the sea. *The coast was dotted with fishing villages.*

current—a mass of liquid or gas that is moving in one direction. *The current pulled us farther out to sea.*

tide—the rise and fall of the ocean caused by the pull of the moon and the sun. *When the tide fell, many shells were left on the beach.*

One hot August afternoon, Glenda Lennon dived off a boat into the ocean. After a few moments Glenda called to her husband, "Robert, the current is starting to pull me out!"

Robert dived into the warm water off the coast of Florida. Spunky, their poodle, jumped in too. Robert was next to Glenda in a minute. But the little dog was swept away by the tide. Glenda begged Robert to save Spunky. Robert swam to the dog and grabbed him. Then he turned back toward Glenda. He couldn't believe his eyes. Glenda was now in the distance. It took all his strength to reach her.

Using skills and strategies

Making predictions

When you read, you understand and remember more if you think ahead. One way to think ahead is to predict what will happen next in a story. Your prediction should be based on what you have read and what you already know.

In "Alone in the Ocean," you know that Glenda, Robert, and Spunky are in the water. You know strong currents are around them. You also know that the title of the article is "Alone in the Ocean." Who do you think will be alone—Glenda, Robert, Spunky, or all three of them? Write your prediction in the margin above.

Robert was a strong swimmer. He had been a water-safety teacher and had swum in many races. Even so, he couldn't pull both Glenda and Spunky against the current. The boat was too far away now. Robert would have to swim to the boat alone. Then he would drive it back and rescue Glenda.

"Stay here," Robert told Glenda. "Just relax as much as you can. Don't fight the water at all. Raise your head when you need to breathe."

Oceans can have strong currents. You should be a strong swimmer to swim in the ocean.

For hours Robert swam toward the boat. He could not see it at all now. The sun was setting in the west. Robert knew his boat would be in the east. He swam with the sun to his back.

Finally the current stopped pulling Robert. He swam as hard as he could. Robert finally reached the boat. It was six hours after he had begun swimming. Robert started the engine. Then he got on the radio and asked for help. He knew he was too tired to search for Glenda alone.

Boat owners came. The police came. A fleet of shrimp boats searched for Glenda. Soon the black waters were bright with searchlights. Airplanes dropped flares onto the water. But they found nothing.

Using skills and strategies

Making predictions

Now we know the meaning of the title. Both Glenda and Robert have spent time alone in the ocean. Glenda and her dog still are alone. In spite of all the people searching, no one has found them. How do you think Glenda is doing? Write your prediction in the margin above.

Meanwhile, Glenda struggled alone in the ocean. While the sun had shone, she had been sure Robert would return. But as the sky darkened, she worried. Spunky sensed her fear. He clawed at Glenda and climbed onto her shoulders. His weight pushed Glenda under the water. To calm Spunky, Glenda held him at arm's length. Soon he clawed her again. He climbed onto her shoulders. Glenda spoke softly to him. She cradled him in her arms. It did no good. He kept climbing onto her shoulders.

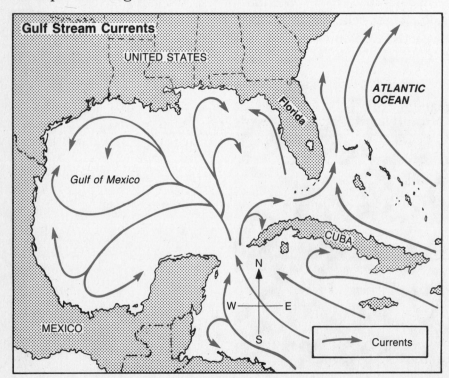

Gulf Stream Currents

UNITED STATES

ATLANTIC OCEAN

Florida

Gulf of Mexico

CUBA

N
W   E
S

Currents

MEXICO

This map of currents shows how difficult it was to predict which way Glenda drifted.

Glenda grew weaker. She could no longer keep both of them afloat. With tears in her eyes, Glenda set Spunky free. She could not watch what she knew was happening to him.

Thinking about Spunky made Glenda feel bad. Thinking about Robert made her worry. Her problems grew when a storm started. Lightning hit the black water around her. The thunder was loud. Glenda was cold. She became sleepy.

Glenda's snorkel kept her alive during the storm. Its lower tube was in her mouth. Its upper tube rose above her head. When waves washed over her, the opening remained above water. Glenda could breathe in fresh air. After the storm, she rested her face on the water. Again, the snorkel remained above water. It allowed her to keep breathing.

Suddenly Glenda heard the sound of an airplane. A flare dropped from the sky. "It's a plane looking for me," thought Glenda. She swam to the flare a hundred yards away. She waved it wildly in the air. "Here I am!" Glenda shouted. "I'm right here! HELP!" The pilot looked below but saw nothing. He flew on. With each passing hour, Glenda grew weaker. She feared she might never be found.

In the morning, Duncan MacRae joined the search. He had spent almost 50 years around the Gulf waters. MacRae knew these waters better than anyone else. He knew which way the currents ran. He knew what winds blow across the water. MacRae knew the water was too shallow for sharks to enter. If Glenda had stayed afloat, she was alive.

Using skills and strategies

Making predictions

MacRae knows the Gulf waters better than anyone else in the search party. This is a good sign. Based on what you have read, how do you think MacRae will search? Write your prediction in the margin. Then check your prediction.

MacRae went to the place where the Lennons' boat was the day before. He let his own boat drift there awhile. He tried to think what had happened to Glenda. MacRae knew that the flow of the current had been about nine miles per hour the day before. When the tide came in that night, it would have swept Glenda toward shore. Now it would be taking her back out again. The west wind also would have taken her in that direction.

MacRae and two other men searched to the northwest. They saw many flashes in the water. None of them was Glenda. The boat raced instead toward bottles, tin cans, and old crab traps. MacRae knew they could easily pass Glenda. So they went over the same waters a few times.

After a while, even MacRae's search party began to lose hope. Glenda had been in the water for 20 hours. That was a long time for anyone to survive in a strong current— even a strong swimmer. Glenda was not a strong swimmer. The group did not think she had survived. The search for Glenda Lennon drew to a close.

On the way back, two people in the boat saw another flash. They no longer thought it could be Glenda. But they headed toward it anyway. Soon they saw a small, thin arm. They had found Glenda! MacRae got into a small boat. He reached into the ocean and pulled Glenda into the boat. She could not move, but she was alive! "Thank God," she whispered as she began crying. MacRae wrapped Glenda in a blanket. He was crying, too.

"I want to go to my husband," Glenda finally said. "Is he still alive?"

"Yes, he is," said MacRae. "And he is going to be one happy fellow when he sees who we have aboard." MacRae turned the boat toward the east. He drove as fast as he could. He knew how tricky the Gulf currents could be.

Think About What You've Read

Important ideas

1. What was Robert's plan to rescue Glenda? Why didn't it work?

_____

_____

_____

2. Why do you think Glenda was able to stay afloat so long?

_____

_____

_____

3. Why do you think that MacRae was able to find Glenda?

_____

_____

Use what you've learned before

4. Pretend you are teaching a class about surviving in the ocean. What would you want to teach your students?

_____

_____

Important word meanings

Write the letter of the word from Column 2 that completes the phrase in Column 1.

Column 1	Column 2
_____ 1. high and low	a. coast
_____ 2. a difficult	b. tide
_____ 3. the land along the	c. current
_____ 4. a swift	d. challenge

Using skills and strategies

Read the predictions you wrote as you read "Alone in the Ocean." Below them, write down your reasons for making the predictions.

Writing

Pretend that you are Glenda Lennon and you want to thank the people who searched for you. Your thank-you letter will appear in the local newspaper. On a sheet of paper, write what you would say.

Your important ideas

Look back over the article. Write down one idea that seems to be the most important one to you—the one idea that you would like to remember.

_____

_____

Your important words

Look back at the words you have learned as you read "Alone in the Ocean." Write down the word or words that you think are most important—that you would like to remember.

_____

Hijacked!

What do you already know?
Write down three facts you already know about hijacking of airplanes. Work with a partner, if you like.

1. _____

2. _____

3. _____

Make predictions
Look at the pictures and the headings—the words in large type—in "Hijacked!" Then write down three facts that you think you will learn as you read.

1. _____

2. _____

3. _____

Set your purpose for reading
Write down one thing you hope to find out about terrorists or airline hijacking as you read this article.

_____

_____

_____

Learn important words
Study the meanings of the words below and how they are used in sentences. Knowing these words might help you as you read "Hijacked!"

barrier—something that blocks movement. *The barrier kept the pilot from landing the plane.*

hijacker—person who takes control of an airplane by force. *The hijacker did not care about the other passengers when he took over the plane.*

terrorist—person who uses force to achieve goals. *The terrorist hurt many people with the bomb.*

On June 14, 1985, a flight took off from Athens, Greece. Captain John Testrake was the pilot. He turned the plane toward Rome. Uli Derickson was a flight attendant. She turned her attention toward her work. There were 153 people on the plane. Many were Americans on vacation.

Suddenly there was shouting on board. Someone pushed Uli Derickson against the cockpit door. A man held a gun at her head. Another man held a live hand grenade. Both men shouted at Uli in Arabic. She did not understand them. She told them she spoke English and German.

One of the men yelled in German, "Open the cockpit door. We come to die."

Using skills and strategies

Using a dictionary

Often in your reading you come across new words. You may be unsure of their meanings. This makes it hard to understand what you read. A dictionary will help you.

A dictionary lists words in alphabetical order. For each word, it lists one or more meanings. Look up the words *cockpit* and *grenade* in a dictionary. For each word, choose the meaning that makes sense in the paragraphs above. Write that meaning in the margin.

As you read this article, circle any words that are not clear to you.

The two hijackers entered the cockpit. Their guns were pointed at the captain. They had the grenades with them. The men shouted, "Beirut, Beirut!" One hijacker beat a passenger with a pistol. Captain Testrake did not argue.

Hijackers hold Captain Testrake at gunpoint in the cockpit and tell him where to fly.

17

He wanted everyone alive when his was over. He turned the plane toward Beirut, Lebanon. The hijackers ran up and down the aisles beating more passengers.

Derickson knew Arab men respect the role of mother. She told the hijackers she had a seven-year-old son. She also knew some of the teachings of the Koran, the Muslim holy book. Derickson let the hijackers know she was interested in their country. She made tea. When the hijackers took the tea, Derickson knew she had won their respect.

After that, Derickson could sometimes help the passengers. For example, one hijacker started beating an American. Derickson ran up and held the arms of the hijacker. He was surprised. Derickson looked the hijacker in the eye and told him to stop. He did.

Derickson couldn't stop the hijackers from beating every passenger. The hijackers kept beating one American sailor. His U.S. Navy boat had shelled the hills near Beirut the year before. Many Arabs were killed by the shelling.

The terrorists wanted Israel to free Arabs held in Israel. They planned to keep the passengers until the Arabs were freed. Israel did not want to do what the terrorists asked. They did not want to look as if they were giving in.

Captain Testrake landed in Beirut. Nobody there would talk to the terrorists. In Beirut, Derickson talked the hijackers into freeing the old women and children. The other passengers forced themselves to stay calm. They knew their lives depended on not making the hijackers angry.

The terrorists decided to go to Algeria. Testrake flew the plane there. Still no one would talk to the terrorists.

This map shows Algeria and Lebanon. The hijacked plane traveled back and forth between these two countries.

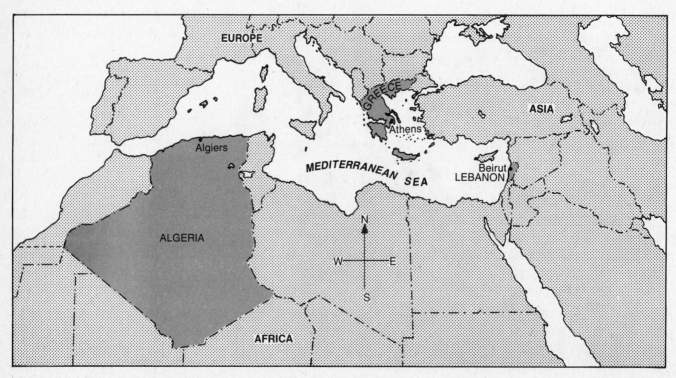

The terrorists told Testrake to fly back to Beirut. The army in Beirut placed barriers on the airport runways. If the plane tried to land, it would crash into the barriers. The plane was almost out of fuel. Captain Testrake told the control tower the plane would crash if he didn't land. He was landing. The crew got the passengers ready for a crash landing. The army then decided to clear the runways.

On the ground, the hijackers talked to the control tower. The terrorists wanted some Muslim leaders in Beirut to join them on the plane. These leaders didn't want to be part of the hijacking. The terrorists said they would begin shooting passengers unless the Muslim leaders came. They pushed the American sailor into the open doorway and killed him.

Soon the Muslim leaders entered the plane. They took control away from the two hijackers. The killing ended. Yet the passengers and crew were still prisoners.

The Muslim leaders had some passengers taken from the plane. At first these passengers thought they would be killed. Instead, they were hidden in Beirut in small groups. A ten-year-long war raged around them. They heard shooting daily.

The next morning, the terrorists demanded a return to Algeria. There they freed Uli Derickson and 55 passengers. The remaining 36 hostages were all American men.

Using skills and strategies

Using a dictionary

The word *hostage* has not been used in the article before. Do you know what the word means? If you don't, look up its meaning in a dictionary. What word in the third paragraph on this page has almost the same meaning as *hostage*? Write that word in the margin.

The next morning the airplane flew back to Beirut. Testrake worried about the airplane. He couldn't keep flying it without doing any repair work. There would be engine trouble soon.

Testrake decided to fake engine trouble. On the way to Beirut, the crew turned off one engine. Then they turned off another engine, and another. When they finally landed, the hijackers thought the plane couldn't fly any more.

Now the hijackers sent the rest of the passengers into Beirut. Only Captain Testrake and his co-pilot were left on the plane.

In their hiding places, the hostages encouraged each other. Each group chose leaders. Many hostages looked for ways to escape. But they knew that an escape would put the others in worse danger. So they waited. They trusted that leaders in the Middle East and the U.S. would rescue them.

Two of the American hostages are allowed to speak at a press conference in Beirut.

Some hostages got to know their guards. In fact, some guards were friendly. They wanted to keep the Americans safe. But they wanted to keep them as hostages until the Arabs in Israel were free. Often the hostages heard radio news. They learned what was being done to free them. They tried to be patient.

For 16 days the plane sat in the Beirut airport. The hostages waited in their small rooms. At last, the scattered groups were brought together in a schoolyard. They knew that the government leaders were coming to an agreement! Later they learned that Israel would free the Arab prisoners. Now they knew that they were on their way home.

Think About What You've Read

Important ideas
1. Why did terrorists hijack the airplane?

_____

_____

2. Why did the pilot follow the hijackers' orders?

_____

_____

3. How did Uli Derickson help the passengers?

_____

_____

4. How do you think our country should deal with terrorists? Give reasons for your answer.

_____

_____

Use what you've learned before
5. How was the rescue of the hostages different from the one for Glenda Lennon?

_____

_____

Important word meanings
Write a synonym—a word that means almost the same thing—for each of the words listed below.

1. barrier _____

2. hijacker _____

3. mountaineering _____

4. terrorist _____

Using skills and strategies
There are words in "Hijacked!" that are not easy to say correctly. Find a word you are not sure how to pronounce. Circle it. Look it up in your dictionary. The pronunciation comes after the word you looked up. Write the pronunciation in the margin on this page.

Writing
Imagine that you were one of the passengers on the plane. On a sheet of paper, write a letter to a friend. Tell what happened during the hijacking.

Your important ideas
Look back over the article. Write down one idea that seems to be the most important one to you—the idea that you would like to remember.

_____

_____

Your important words
Look at the words you have learned as you read "Hijacked!" Write down the word or words that you think are most important—that you would like to remember.

_____

To Save His Men

What do you already know?

Write down three facts that you already know about the land around the South Pole. You might write the name for the land, the weather there, and what it would be like to try to survive there. Work with a partner, if you like.

1. _____
2. _____
3. _____

Make predictions

Look at the pictures in the article. Then write down three things you think you will learn as you read "To Save His Men."

1. _____
2. _____
3. _____

Set your purpose for reading

Write down one thing you hope to find out about Antarctica, shipwrecks, or explorers as you read this article.

_____

_____

_____

Learn important words

Study the meanings of the words below and how they are used in sentences. Knowing these words might help you as you read "To Save His Men."

capsize—to turn bottom-side up; to overturn. *When the storm came, we feared that the boat would capsize.*

gale—a wind that blows at a speed of 32 to 63 miles per hour. *People could hardly stand because of the gale.*

whaler—a large ship, used for hunting whales. *Whalers were often the only ships that passed near the South Pole.*

Antarctica is the icy land around the South Pole. The temperature stays about 70 degrees below zero. Ice mountains and snow cover the ground all year. Sea ice floats in the waters around Antarctica.

By the late 1890s, explorers began to go to Antarctica. Once they arrived, helping them was impossible. They didn't have airplanes. There were no good radios for sending messages. Snow tractors didn't exist. No one was nearby. The explorers were on their own in the bitter cold.

Yet people wanted to go to Antarctica. In 1899, ten men from Great Britain spent a winter there. Eleven years later, Ernest Shackleton, a British explorer, got within 97 miles of the South Pole. In 1911, Roald Amundsen of Norway reached the South Pole.

The explorers kept coming. Then, in 1915, Ernest Shackleton tried to cross Antarctica from coast to coast. In the history of this frozen land, no other story matches his.

Using skills and strategies

Making predictions

You have already begun learning to make predictions as you read. What prediction would you make here?

So far the article has been about early explorers of Antarctica. The last sentence says that no story matches Ernest Shackleton's. You might predict that the rest of the article will be about Shackleton.

This picture shows one of the first men to reach the South Pole.

Four hundred miles from Antarctica, ice stopped Shackleton's boat. He and his crew waited for winter to pass. Then, after nine months in icy water, their wooden ship cracked! The men took their supplies and three wooden lifeboats off the ship. Two days later the ship sank. Shackleton had no hope of crossing Antarctica now. He thought only of saving his men.

For the next five months the men pushed northwest. In April of 1916, they reached Elephant Island. They were weak. Food was running out. Winter was coming. No one lived on Elephant Island. Gales and snowstorms made living there difficult. Shackleton knew that whalers came by the island. But none of the whaling ships would find them before winter. And they couldn't survive the winter on the island. They had too few supplies.

Shackleton formed a dangerous plan. It was their only hope. He asked four men to go with him to the whaling station 800 miles away. To reach it they would have to cross some of the stormiest seas in the world. Snowstorms and gales were common. Yet, every one of Shackleton's men asked to go! He chose the strongest men to go with him. They set out in the best lifeboat. As they left, the men on shore broke up the last two lifeboats to build shelters. Now they were stuck on Elephant Island. They would have to wait for Shackleton to come back.

Using skills and strategies

Making predictions

All of these men are in danger. The men on the island have very little food and shelter. The explorers in the lifeboat are trying to cross 800 miles of stormy, cold sea. What dangers will the men in the boat face? How can they survive? Write your predictions in the margin.

Shackleton's little boat was alone in the ocean. For four days it passed through storms. On the fifth day, wind and waves rose stronger than any of the men had ever faced. Ice formed on the deck and on the mast. Shackleton knew the ice would make the boat top-heavy. Soon it would capsize! The men were full of fear. They chipped away at the ice that kept forming. They threw supplies into the ocean. They worked hard for two days. Then, on the seventh day, the wind died. The sea calmed. Hope returned.

The little boat sailed on calmly for three more days. Suddenly a gale struck! Huge waves formed. "Bail for your lives!" cried Shackleton. The men bailed water over the side. Finally the storm passed. The little boat had survived again. But the men were almost out of drinking water. Soon they would die of thirst!

At noon on the 14th day, Shackleton sighted land! The coast was rocky, however, with steep cliffs. There was no

The wooden ship *Endurance* cracks and sinks. This picture was taken by a crew member in 1915.

place to bring the boat ashore. The thirsty men spent another night at sea.

That night a strong gale arose! Water poured into the boat. The wind drove them back out to sea. The men, tired and weak, were about to give up. They were sure the boat would capsize this time. Then the wind died. They were safe again. After a second night still at sea, Shackleton found a narrow gap in the barrier of rocks. The boat sailed to shore. The explorers drank fresh water from a stream.

The tired group camped in a cave. Behind them were mountains 4,000 feet high. No one had ever crossed these mountains. In the morning, Shackleton chose the two strongest men. They started climbing. The other men stayed in the cave. They had enough food for a few days.

Shackleton and his men had no tents for camping. If they stopped climbing, they would freeze to death. So the men climbed through the night. In the morning they heard a strange whistling sound. Shackleton looked at his watch. It was 7:00 A.M. Had the whistle come from the whaling station? Was it calling the whalers? The three small figures climbed the final ridge. Below them were huts and people! They were safe.

Using skills and strategies

Making predictions

What prediction would you make here? Now that Shackleton is safe, what will he do next? How will he get back to his men? Write your prediction in the margin.

The next day whalers rescued the two men on the other side of the island. But Shackleton was worried. How would he reach his crew on Elephant Island?

For the next 100 days, Shackleton and two of his men tried to reach Elephant Island. They had only a small whaling boat. They got as close as 60 miles from the island. Then ice and snowstorms forced them to turn back!

In a stronger boat, Shackleton tried again. This time, he got to within 18 miles of Elephant Island. Again the ice forced him back. A third rescue party set out and also failed.

Finally the government of Chile lent Shackleton a better boat. This time he reached Elephant Island! Shackleton looked through his binoculars. He counted the tiny figures on the island. Then he let out a cry of joy. All his men were alive! Each morning they had prepared to be rescued that day. They had never lost hope that Shackleton would return.

Think About What You've Read

Important ideas

1. What did Ernest Shackleton plan to do in the Antarctic?

_____

_____

2. How was the adventure Shackleton had different from the one he planned?

_____

_____

3. Based on what you have read, what kind of man do you think Shackleton was?

_____

_____

_____

26

4. How were Captain Testrake and Ernest Shackleton alike?

_____

_____

_____

Important word meanings

Find a place in the article where each of these words is used: *barrier, capsize, coast, gale*. Underline those words in the article. Then write a sentence using each word. For example, for *capsize*, you might find a place where the men feared the boat would capsize. You could write a sentence telling whether or not the boat capsized.

_____

_____

_____

_____

Using skills and strategies

Reread the predictions you made as you read "To Save His Men." Circle the ones that turned out to be correct.

Writing

Imagine that you are Ernest Shackleton or one of the people in his crew. Pretend that you keep a journal of your adventures in Antarctica. Choose one part of the journey. On a sheet of paper, write a journal entry about that part of the journey.

Your important ideas

Look back over the article. Write down one idea that seems to be the most important one to you—the one idea that you would like to remember.

_____

_____

Your important words

Look back at the words you have learned as you read "To Save His Men." Write down the word or words you think are most important—that you would like to remember.

_____

_____

Flying in a Balloon

What do you already know?

Write down three facts you already know about flying in a hot-air or helium balloon. Work with a partner, if you like.

1. _____

2. _____

3. _____

Make predictions

Look at the pictures in the article. Then write down three things you think you will learn as you read this article.

1. _____

2. _____

3. _____

Set your purpose for reading

Write down one thing you hope to find out about balloon flying as you read this article.

_____

_____

_____

Learn important words

Study the meanings of the words below and how they are used in sentences. Knowing these words might help you as you read this article.

altitude—height above the earth's surface. *There is less oxygen in the air at a high altitude.*

solo—alone. *The pilot was flying solo, so he had to count on his own judgment and skills.*

sonic boom—a loud sound, as of an explosion, caused by planes traveling near the speed of sound. *Pilots try to avoid creating sonic booms over towns.*

"You just have to go for it. That's the American way," said Joseph Kittinger. He has been "going for it" all his life. Kittinger took up ballooning as a young man in the air force. He tested the effects of high altitudes on pilots. In one test, Kittinger jumped from a balloon 20 miles above the Earth. He was almost in outer space. He breathed bottled oxygen and wore a space suit. Kittinger fell faster than 600 miles per hour. He broke the sound barrier. He fell 16 miles before opening his parachute.

This fall broke three records. It was the highest balloon flight on record. It was the longest free fall ever. It was the fastest anyone had ever traveled without a machine.

Ballooning is a popular sport. Most balloons used for sport are filled with hot air.

Using skills and strategies

Main idea

You know that a paragraph is a group of sentences about one idea. That idea is the main idea of the paragraph. For example, reread paragraph 1 on page 29. Its main idea is how Joseph Kittinger "goes for it."

Often the first sentence states the main idea. Does the first sentence lead to every other sentence? If so, it states the main idea. Reread paragraph 2 on page 29. The first sentence states the main idea. It says that Kittinger's fall broke three records. The other sentences describe those records.

In four of the six paragraphs below, the first sentence states the main idea. Underline these sentences that state the main idea.

"Life is an adventure, and I'm an adventurer," said Kittinger. On September 14, 1984, Kittinger began his solo flight across the Atlantic in a balloon. Before this, six balloon pilots had tried to cross the Atlantic alone. None had made it. Two had died trying.

When Kittinger set out across the Atlantic, he wanted to break three records. He wanted to make the first solo balloon flight across the Atlantic. He wanted to set the world record for distance and the world record for time.

Kittinger flew a helium balloon as tall as a ten-story building. Helium is a gas that is lighter than air. A helium balloon can fly higher than a hot-air balloon. It can stay up for a longer time. A boat followed the balloon from below. The people in the boat could save Kittinger if he landed in the ocean.

Weather was important to Kittinger on his flight. He had to know how currents of air moved at different heights. People on the ground told him how fast wind currents were flowing at different altitudes. They also told him the direction of the currents. Kittinger needed to be at an altitude where the air flowed east. Also, the current he chose could not move too fast.

Only two problems came up. The biggest one arose as Kittinger lit his gasoline stove. It burst into flames! For years, Kittinger had been planning in his mind every detail of the flight. Now his planning paid off. He quickly put out the fire. Kittinger's second problem was smaller. Sonic booms from high-flying aircraft kept slamming into his balloon. He says they sounded like 50 tons of dynamite going off.

Kittinger slept very little during the flight. He had to keep an eye on altitude and direction. He kept in contact with the boat crew and others guiding him. To stay alert, he breathed bottled oxygen about half of the time.

Finally Kittinger reached the other side of the Atlantic. But he didn't land right away. He wanted to break the distance record. After 83 hours and 40 minutes in the air, Kittinger neared Italy. Thunderstorms were above him. They could destroy his balloon. Forests lay below. They would be difficult to land in.

Kittinger chose the forest. He counted on his past experience to help him. Ground-level winds were gusting. Kittinger worried about landing in power lines, on highways, and in the trees. He crash-landed on a hilltop. Finally, the record-breaking balloonist had landed!

The force of the landing broke a bone in his right foot. "It's embarrassing, really," Kittinger said.

Woodcutters carried Kittinger to a helicopter. It took him to a nearby hospital. He was treated there.

Kittinger had made the first solo crossing of the Atlantic Ocean in a balloon. He had also broken the distance record for flying solo in a balloon. Kittinger went about 1,000 miles farther than the former record holder. He had traveled 3,535 miles. Kittinger had "gone for it." And he had done things no one had ever done.

Using skills and strategies

Main idea

The main idea of a paragraph is not always stated in the first sentence. Some main ideas are stated in the last sentence of their paragraphs. For example, look at the next paragraph. Its main idea is that you may want to become a balloonist.

The main idea in the last paragraph in this story on page 32 is stated in its last sentence. Find that paragraph and underline the sentence that states the main idea.

Becoming a balloonist

Perhaps you like challenges, as Joseph Kittinger does. You may like the excitement and beauty of a balloon flight. Then you may want to become a balloonist.

Most balloons used for sport are hot-air balloons. They cost a lot less to fill than gas balloons. It costs about $3,000 to fill a helium balloon. Hot-air balloons can be filled for about $20 using a burner!

To learn more about hot-air ballooning, look for helpful balloon pilots near your city or town. Every balloonist needs a ground crew. If you become part of a crew, your balloonist may pay you with flying lessons.

Members of the ground crew perform several tasks. They fill the balloon. They use fans to blow in cold air. Next, they heat the air. They do this with a hand-held burner. When the air is hot, the balloon rises into the air. Then the ground crew follows it in a truck. When it comes down, the crew takes it apart and packs it in the truck.

Ground crews help prepare a balloon for flight.

You can begin training to be a balloon pilot at age 14. A 16-year-old can apply for a pilot's license. As a student pilot, you need at least ten hours of flying time and ground training. You must pass a written test. You fly at least two flights that are 30 minutes long. One flight must be a solo flight. Finally, you take a special test flight. When you complete all the requirements, you will be a balloon pilot!

Think About What You've Read

Important ideas

1. What experiences did Kittinger have as a balloonist before crossing the Atlantic?

_____

_____

2. What is Kittinger's Atlantic flight remembered for?

_____

_____

_____

3. What must you do to become a balloon pilot?

_____

_____

_____

Use what you've learned before
4. Why do you think Kittinger's plans were more
   successful than Shackleton's?

_____

_____

Important word meanings

Altitude and _currents_ affected Kittinger's flights. What
other words in the article are things that affected Kittinger's
flights? Write the words on the lines below. Write their
meanings next to them.

_____

_____

_____

Using skills and strategies

On a sheet of paper, write a paragraph about something
in "Flying in a Balloon" that you liked. State the main idea
of your paragraph in your last sentence.

Writing

For years Kittinger planned the adventure he wanted to
have—crossing the Atlantic in a balloon. On a sheet of
paper, describe an adventure you would like. How might
you plan for it?

Your important ideas

Look back over the article. Write down one idea that
seems to be the most important one to you—the one idea
that you would like to remember.

_____

_____

Your important words

Look back at the words you have learned as you read
"Flying in a Balloon." Write down the word or words that
you think are most important—that you would most like to
remember.

_____

_____

Reviewing What You Have Learned

Some facts and ideas you have learned

You learned many important facts and ideas as you read about survival. A few of them are listed below. Add your own important ideas to the end of this list. You can look back at the "Your important ideas" section of each lesson to remember the ideas you wrote down.

- Facing challenges helps people feel confident.
- Ocean tides and currents can carry swimmers out to sea.
- Terrorists use force to gain their goals.
- Ernest Shackleton's courage and concern saved his men from death in the Antarctic.
- Joseph Kittinger was the first person to fly solo in a balloon across the Atlantic Ocean.

_____

_____

_____

Some word meanings you have learned

Here are some of the important words you learned in the articles you read. Make sure you understand their meanings. Then add important words of your own. You can look back at the "Your important words" section of each lesson to remember the words you wrote down.

altitude—height above the Earth's surface. *The wind blew harder as the balloon gained altitude.*

gale—a wind that blows at a speed of 32 to 63 miles per hour. *People could hardly stand up because of the gale.*

_____

_____

_____

Purposes for reading

Look back at the section at the beginning of every lesson called "Set your purpose for reading." Think about the purposes you set for reading the articles in this cluster. Choose a purpose that you achieved by reading one of the articles. On a separate sheet of paper, write the purpose. Explain how reading the article helped you learn what you hoped to learn.

_____

_____

Using skills and strategies

Examine the first four paragraphs of "To Save His Men" on page 23. Find a paragraph in which the main idea is stated in the first sentence. Underline the sentence. Now find a paragraph in which the main idea is stated in the last sentence. Underline that sentence.

On the lines below, write the sentences you underlined.

_____

_____

_____

_____

Writing: personal opinion

Choose an article you liked from this cluster. Write how you feel about the events in it. Did you think some people in the article behaved badly? Did you think someone made a poor decision? Who earned your respect? On a sheet of paper, write what you think.

Revising

Go back and read what you have written about your feelings. Did you use complete sentences? Did you group sentences about the same idea into paragraphs? Do your paragraphs have a main idea? Revise what you wrote.

Activities

1. If you are interested in Outward Bound programs, write to the following address. When the information arrives, share it with the class.

   > Outward Bound USA
   > 384 Field Point Road
   > Greenwich, Conn. 06830

   If you prefer, call this toll-free number: 800-243-8520.
2. Look up ocean tides in books about the ocean or in an encyclopedia. Find out why the tides come and go. Then plan a demonstration for the class. For example, you might use a globe, two balls (for the sun and the moon), and bowls of water. You can fill and empty the bowls to demonstrate how the tides come and go.
3. Shackleton's men would not have survived if they had not found food in the ocean. Read about the animals that live near Antarctica. Find out how they survive the cold. Report what you learn to the class.
4. If you are interested in ballooning, read *Ballooning* by Carole S. Briggs (Lerner Publications Company, 1986). It tells about hot-air balloons, gas balloons, and how you can get into ballooning.

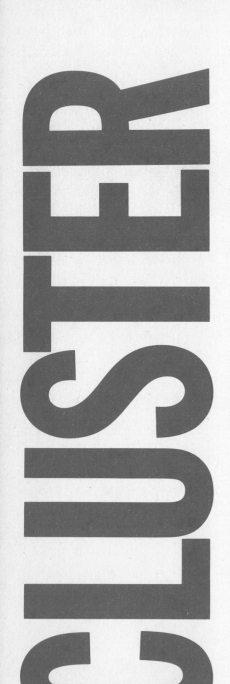

Monsters

Read and learn about monsters

Monsters! Children have nightmares about them. For centuries, people told myths about them. Great authors have written about them. Now we watch thrilling movies about them and shiver with fear. Some people even search for monsters.

Almost all monster stories are scary. But the monsters are not all alike. Some are strange beasts that live on Earth. Some come from outer space. Others were made by humans. Still others were animals or people that changed into hideous monsters.

You don't have to be a child to be afraid of monsters. And you don't have to be crazy to love them.

What do you already know about monsters?

Talk about what you know. Get together with a group of students to talk about what you already know about monsters. Here are some questions to help you get started.

1. What are some of the most famous monsters?
2. Do you know of any monsters that might be real?
3. Which monster movies have you seen? How are they alike?

Write about what you know. Think about the monsters you have read about or seen in movies. Write three things you already know about these monsters.

_____

_____

_____

Make predictions

Read the titles of the articles in Cluster 2 and look at the picture on page 37. Write down three things that you think you'll learn by reading these articles about monsters.

1. _____

2. _____

3. _____

Start to learn new word meanings

All of the words listed below are used in the three paragraphs on page 36. Study the meanings of these words as you read about monsters.

century—one hundred years. *People have read about Frankenstein for over a century.*

myth—a story that explains something in nature. *One myth told how a giant sea monster sank ships.*

hideous—very ugly. *The man changed into a hideous beast when the moon was full.*

Learn new skills and strategies

In this cluster you will learn about finding the implied main idea of a paragraph. This strategy will help you discover important information. You also will learn about finding details and reading pictures.

Gather new information

By the end of this cluster, you will have learned the answers to these questions.

1. Why have people loved monster stories for hundreds of years?
2. How did some of the great monster stories come to be written?
3. What are some of the reasons for and against believing in monsters or strange creatures?
4. What are some tricks film makers use in monster movies?

Monster Myths Through the Ages

What do you already know?

Tell something about two monsters in stories from long ago. Work with a partner, if you like.

1. _____

2. _____

3. _____

Make predictions

Look at the pictures and the headings in the article. Then write down three things that you think you will learn about as you read this article.

1. _____

2. _____

3. _____

Set your purpose for reading

Write down one thing you hope to find out about monster myths as you read this article.

_____

_____

Learn important words

Study the meanings of the words below and the way they are used in sentences. Knowing these words might help you as you read this article.

myth—a story that explains something in nature. *In one myth, a monster could kill people by looking at them.*

fantasy—something imagined or made up, not real. *The story of a monster from Mars is only fantasy.*

symbol—a thing that makes people think of a certain idea. *A monster can be a symbol of danger or death.*

evidence—something that makes people believe a statement is true. *He thought the bones were evidence that monsters still lived.*

Once upon a time, a strange thing happened: a rooster laid an egg. Through the grass came a snake. It wrapped itself around the egg. It kept the egg warm. After a time, the shell began to crack. The snake moved off into the dark grass. Then the shell fell away. Out came a scary creature. It had the body, wings, and feet of a rooster. But the tail twisted and turned. It was the tail of a curling snake. The head was the head of a snake. The creature had a long, darting tongue. Its eyes were the awful eyes of a toad.

This was the myth of the basilisk. The basilisk was a very harmful monster. <u>Any plant it touched would dry up and die. Any rock it touched would break. Even a basilisk's breath could kill a person. In fact, just a look from the beast could kill.</u> <u>A man on horseback could stab a basilisk with a spear. But then poison would climb the spear, and the man would die.</u> So would the horse. There was only one way to kill a basilisk. That was with a mirror. If the beast looked in the mirror, its own glance would kill it.

The basilisk is part snake and part rooster. Myths say one look from the beast can kill.

Using skills and strategies

Finding details

Details are the ideas and other information that support the main idea in a paragraph. For example, if you say "It's been a bad day," you could support that idea with details. The details might be that you missed the bus and lost your backpack.

The main idea in the paragraph you just read is that the basilisk was thought to be very harmful. Five other sentences in the paragraph are underlined. Each of the five sentences is a supporting detail. Read the paragraph once again. Number the supporting details.

The sphinx of Egypt had the body
of a lion and head of a human.

The monster appears

People in Europe believed in basilisks for hundreds of
years. In 1587, in Warsaw, Poland, two small girls were
found dead in a cellar. Everyone felt sure a basilisk had
killed them. No one, however, dared to search for the
monster. Someone had an idea. There was a criminal who
was to be put to death soon for his crimes. What did it
matter if a basilisk killed him? The criminal put on a
leather suit covered with mirrors. He went into the cellar.

When he came up again, he was carrying something. It
looked like a plain dead snake. But could it be a basilisk?
Who knew? Few people had ever seen a real one. Those
who *had* seen one had died. At last, the king's doctor was
called in. He studied the beast. Yes, he said; it *was* a
basilisk. The monster had struck again!

How are monster myths alike?

The myth of the basilisk is just one of hundreds of
monster tales. For thousands of years, people have told
such tales. In many tales the monster was made up of two
kinds of animals. The basilisk, for example, was such a
creature of fantasy. Sometimes the beast was part animal,
part human. The sphinx of Egypt was this type. It had the
body of a lion and the head of a man or woman. People
believed in these monsters. They believed the monsters
were very powerful. They also believed the monsters were
very harmful.

In monster tales, people told of awful events. Many of
these events really happened. But they were hard to
understand. A child might fall sick and die. A bad storm
might tear down homes and crops. Lightning might crack
and flash in the dark sky of night. Who could explain such
things? They came without warning. People feared them.

By telling monster tales, people could talk about their fears. They used monsters as symbols. A monster could stand for a harmful force in the world. The force could not be seen, but it made things happen. It might be death. It might be bad luck. It might be human meanness. The tales told that monsters caused these forces. They told how the forces worked.

Truth or fantasy?

People who looked could find evidence that monsters existed. Three thousand years ago, people in the Middle East believed in griffins. These great beasts had wings, feathers, and a head like an eagle's. The beast's body, legs, and paws were like a lion's. It had sharp claws. Its teeth were like spears. Hundreds of years after the first griffin story was told, "evidence" of the beast was still found. People brought strange things to sell in the markets of Europe. They said they were the claws of griffins. Much later, scientists found that those "griffin claws" were really something else. They were tusks or horns from other large animals. But at the time, people thought they were proof that griffins *did* exist.

Modern science has explored more such tales. Some have turned out to be based on fact. For example, sailors often spoke of a huge sea monster. They called it a kraken. It had many arms and could pull a ship down into the sea. Its eyes were two feet across. Tales of the kraken were told for hundreds of years. At last, scientists found that there really *was* such a huge sea animal. It was a giant squid larger than any ever known before. It might not pull down ships. But it had many arms, and it could grow to be more than 70 feet long!

Using skills and strategies

Finding details

The main idea in the paragraph just above is that some monster stories were based on fact. Underline a detail that supports the main idea in the paragraph.

Monsters can take many shapes. Today, scientists believe that most monsters are made up in our dreams.

Today, scientists think that most monster stories are only fantasy. Many other people agree. Yet children still love scary monster tales, and adults often like a good monster movie. In fact, many of us make up monster stories in our dreams. In those dreams, we see our own fears. It seems that our fear of monsters—and our love for them—are part of human nature.

Think About What You've Read

Important ideas

1. List three ways in which the myth of the basilisk was like many other monster myths.

_____

_____

_____

Use what you've learned before

2. Name or describe a monster from a monster movie you have seen or heard about. How is it different from the monsters in myths?

_____

_____

_____

Important word meanings

Fill in each blank in the sentences with one of the words below. Then write a sentence of your own using each vocabulary word.

myth   fantasy   symbol   evidence

1. Eric's favorite _____ is that he's a famous rock star.

_____

2. That _____ explains why we have different seasons.

_____

3. He claimed that his cuts and broken bones were

_____ that he had met and fought with a griffin.

_____

4. The sea monster you saw in your dream is a

_____ of your fear of water.

_____

Using skills and strategies

One important idea in this article is that people have told monster stories for many hundreds of years. Look back at the article and find three sentences that support this idea. Underline those sentences.

Writing

Imagine you're babysitting for a young child. Make up a new monster story to tell him or her. On a separate piece of paper, describe the monster. Make a clear picture of it in words. If you like, draw a picture of it also. Be sure to tell what the monster does that makes it harmful or scary.

Your important ideas

Look back over the article. Write down one idea that seems to be the most surprising or interesting to you—an idea that you would like to remember.

_____

Your important words

Look back at the words you have learned as you read about monster myths. Write down the word or words that you think are most important—that you would like to remember.

_____

Frankenstein: Story of a Lonely Monster

What do you already know?

Write down three things you know about Frankenstein's monster. Work with a partner, if you like.

1. _____

2. _____

3. _____

Make predictions

Look at the pictures and the headings in the article. Then write down three things that you think you will learn as you read this article.

1. _____

2. _____

3. _____

Set your purpose for reading

Write down one or two things you hope to find out about the story of Frankenstein's monster as you read this article.

_____

_____

Learn important words

Study the meanings of the words below and how they are used in sentences. Knowing these words might help you as you read this article.

grief—deep sadness. *Mary was filled with grief after her mother died.*

hideous—very ugly. *The monster in the movie was hideous.*

rage—great anger. *When the monster's sadness turned to rage, it began to kill people.*

menace—serious danger. *Dr. Frankenstein's monster became a menace to human beings.*

Eleven days after Mary Godwin was born, her mother died. The year was 1797; the place was London, England. Mary's father was a famous writer. But he was not a loving man. Mary had to get used to life without love.

When Mary was four, her father remarried. The woman had two children already. Mary might have hoped her life would now be happier. But that was not to be. Her stepmother was kind only to her own children. She treated Mary as an outsider.

Frankenstein: Story of a Lonely Monster

Using skills and strategies

Finding the implied main idea

The main idea is the most important idea of a paragraph. Sometimes that idea is not stated in any one sentence, but is implied, or suggested. That means you need to figure it out. To do that, you must read the whole paragraph and decide what it is about.

The paragraph above, for example, does not state its main idea: Her father's new marriage did not make Mary happy. The main ideas of the next two paragraphs are implied, or not stated. They are written for you in parentheses. Continue to look for main ideas. Sometimes they are stated. Sometimes they are implied.

Mary Shelley

In her grief, Mary grew lonely. Each day she spent hours reading or daydreaming. As a teenager, she began writing down her thoughts. When her stepmother wanted Mary to do chores, Mary resisted. Her father didn't help her. Instead, he sent her away. For two years she lived with other families. (Main idea: Mary was unhappy as a teenager.)

She was seventeen when she came back home. She still was unhappy with her family. So she would take books, paper, and pen. She would go to the cemetery. There she would sit for hours beside her mother's grave. She read or wrote. (Main idea: Reading and writing helped Mary feel better.)

One spring day a famous poet, Percy Shelley, came to meet Mary's father. Soon he was coming to the Godwin house every day to see Mary. Her father was not happy about their friendship. So Shelley and Mary met in secret at her mother's grave. In July, Mary ran away with Shelley. She was not yet 18.

That summer was cold and rainy. One night, Mary and two of Shelley's friends sat by the fire telling ghost stories. Then one of them had an idea. Why didn't each of them write a new ghost story? That would be even more fun!

45

The story is born

Mary took several months to finish her story. The tale was called *Frankenstein*. It wasn't about a ghost. It was about a monster and the man who made him.

In Mary's story, Victor Frankenstein was a young scientist. He longed to know what gave life to a human body. He dreamed of creating life through science.

One dark, rainy night, he made his dream become real. He created a living being. It was eight feet tall, with yellowish skin and long, black hair. Its lips were straight black lines. Its eyes were pale and yellow. They looked as dead as the skin around them. The creature was hideous. Yet it was clearly alive.

Dr. Frankenstein had never dreamed he would create something so hideous. He was upset by the sight of this monster! But the monster was more like a human than Frankenstein thought. It wanted love and understanding. Frankenstein refused to give it those things. Instead, he turned away. The monster had to look elsewhere for love.

Everywhere the monster went, people turned away from it. Like its maker, they were upset by its hideous looks. The monster became lonely and angry. At last, it began to kill. It killed Dr. Frankenstein's brother and then his best friend. Finally, it killed Dr. Frankenstein's wife.

Filled with grief and rage, Dr. Frankenstein saw that his creature had become a menace. He set out to find the monster and kill it. But he died before he could find it. Soon after, the monster saw its maker's dead body. The monster was sad. The only man who might care for it was dead. Now the monster looked forward to its own death. Only death would set the monster free.

The public reaction

Frankenstein was published two years after Mary wrote it. It was a great success. People loved the scary yet sad story.

Some saw Frankenstein's monster as a symbol of modern science. After all, the monster was created by science. But its maker didn't take care of what he had made. The creature then became a menace to other people.

Frankenstein has been the subject of many plays and movies.

Frankenstein became one of the most popular stories of all time. Many plays were made of it. In 1910, the first silent movie of it was made. Since then, more than 30 other Frankenstein movies have been made. They are all based on the story written by a lonely teenage girl.

Think About What You've Read

Important ideas
1. As a child, what did Mary do when she felt sad or lonely?

_____

2. Why do you suppose Frankenstein ignored his monster for so long? Why didn't he try to kill it right away?

_____

_____

3. Do you think Frankenstein's monster still could be a symbol of modern science? Why or why not?

_____

Use what you've learned before
4. Is the story of Frankenstein's monster a myth, like that of the basilisk? Give a reason for your answer.

_____

_____

Important word meanings

Underline a sentence in the article where each of the following words is used. Then write a sentence of your own using at least two of the words below.

grief   hideous   rage   menace

_____

_____

_____

_____

Using skills and strategies

One of the main ideas in the article was that Mary had an unhappy childhood. Look back at the article. Find the four paragraphs that present that idea. Put a check mark (✔) before each of these paragraphs.

Writing

Imagine you write newspaper stories for parents who want to know which movies their children should or should not see. Do you think children under 13 should see the movie _Frankenstein_? Write a paragraph stating your opinion. Give reasons why you think that way, using details from the story. Use a separate sheet of paper.

Your important ideas

Look back over the article. Write down one idea that seems to be the most important one to you—the one idea that you would like to remember.

_____

_____

Your important words

Look back at the words you have learned as you read about Dr. Frankenstein and his monster. Write down the word or words that you think are most important—that you would most like to remember.

_____

_____

Dracula: Monster Behind the Movie

What do you already know?

Dracula was a monster known as a vampire. Write down three things that you know about vampires, Dracula, or even vampire bats. Work with a partner, if you like.

1. _____

2. _____

3. _____

Make predictions

Look at the pictures in the article. Then write down three things that you think you will learn about Dracula.

1. _____

2. _____

3. _____

Set your purpose for reading

Write down one thing you hope to find out about Dracula as you read this article.

_____

_____

Learn important words

Study the meanings of the words below and how they are used in sentences. Knowing these words might help you as you read this article.

classic—a book or movie that is thought to have lasting importance.
  The classic movie scared me as much as it once scared my mom.

stake—a length of wood, pointed at one end. *Dracula was killed when a stake was driven into his heart.*

century—one hundred years. *The story of Dracula is almost a century old.*

original—first. *The original story of Dracula scared me even more than the movie about him.*

Last Friday I watched the late movie on TV. It was called *Dracula*. The movie was made in 1931. Mom had seen it before. "It's a classic," she said. "But I'll warn you—it's scary."

"I can take it," I said.

So I watched it. It was about Count Dracula. He's a vampire. That means he bites people's necks and then drinks their blood. He does this only at night. During the day, he rests—in a coffin. There's only one way to kill him. That's by driving a wooden stake through his heart.

The movie was a little spooky, but it was also corny. There were bats flying around. There were big spider webs. Dracula had greasy black hair and wore lots of dark eye make-up. One thing was just plain funny. To keep Dracula away, people would hold up garlic. That made me laugh.

Using skills and strategies

Finding details

Details are the ideas in a paragraph that support the main idea. If you want to express the idea that it's a bad day to go to the beach, you might support that idea with these details: It's chilly outside. It's going to rain.

The main idea in the last paragraph above was that the writer thought *Dracula* was pretty corny. The details that support the main idea are underlined. Number the supporting details.

Count Dracula in the classic 1931 movie, *Dracula*.

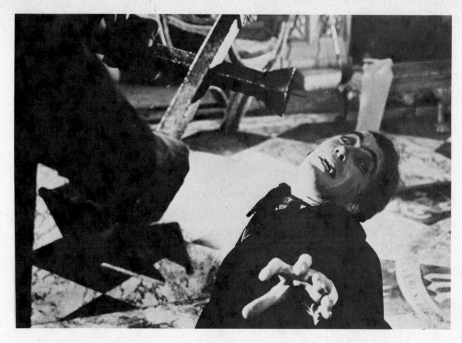

A cross is used to scare off Count Dracula. Legend says the only way to kill Dracula is with a stake through the heart.

On Monday, in school, I ran into my friend Kate. She's an old movie fan; she's seen them all. "Oh, yeah," she said. "It's a classic—one of the greats of this century."

"So I've heard," I said.

"Have you heard about the original Dracula?" she asked.

"What do you mean?" I asked.

"Vlad the Impaler. The real Dracula. Check it out." The bell rang then, and we had to run to class.

That afternoon, I stopped by the library. I was curious, so I looked up Dracula. Boy, what a story *that* was!

Vlad Dracula was a real prince. He lived in eastern Europe five centuries ago. His name, *Dracula*, meant "son of the dragon." He fought against enemies who attacked his country. He was very brave, and he became famous for that. Soon, however, Vlad became mean. He began to kill people just because he didn't like them. He had a favorite way of killing. He would drive a wooden stake through the person's body. That's called impaling. Then he would stick the stake into the ground with the body still on it. That way, everyone was sure to see what he had done. He became known as "Vlad the Impaler." By the time Vlad died, he had killed thousands of people by impaling them.

This true story shook me up quite a bit. Still, I kept reading. It turned out that the movie *Dracula* was based on a book written in 1897. The writer had read about Vlad the Impaler. He also knew that centuries ago, people told tales of creatures called vampires. In those stories, vampires were dead people. They rose from their graves at night. Then they attacked living people and sucked their blood.

No one thought Vlad the Impaler was a vampire. But the author of *Dracula* put the two ideas together. That made a new story. But was it scarier than the true story of Vlad?

That's what I was thinking about when I ran into Kate in gym the next day.

"Hey," I said. "'Vlad the Impaler.'"

"What about him?" she asked.

"Now, he *was* scary! That guy was an animal! He was a *real* monster!"

"I know," said Kate. "That's the thing about movie monsters. They're never as scary as real-life monsters!"

Using skills and strategies

Finding details

One main idea in the last two paragraphs is that Vlad the Impaler was a real monster. Find the details, presented earlier in the article, that support that idea. Circle those details.

Think About What You've Read

Important ideas

1. What was the original reason why Vlad the Impaler became famous?

2. What two stories did the author of *Dracula* use in making up his tale?

3. Do you agree with Kate that people who behave like monsters are scarier than movie monsters? Why?

Use what you've learned before

4. List two ways in which Dracula in the movie and Frankenstein's monster were alike.

5. Name two ways in which Dracula in the movie and Frankenstein's monster were different.

Important word meanings

For each word with a number, choose a similar or related word from the list below. The first one is done for you.

        wooden   award-winner   hundred
                 threat   earliest

1. century _hundred_

2. menace _____

3. classic _____

4. original _____

5. stake _____

Using skills and strategies

Reread the paragraph on page 51 beginning "Vlad Dracula was a real prince." On the lines below, write two details that support the main idea: Dracula was a brave but mean man.

_____

_____

_____

_____

Writing

Imagine you're a police officer. Write a description of Dracula, the movie monster, to be printed on a "Wanted" poster. Describe how he looks and what he does. Also suggest where and how he might be found. You can use the picture on page 50 to help you.

Your important ideas

Look back over the article. Write down one idea that seems to be the most important to you—the one idea that you would like to remember.

_____

_____

Your important words

Look back at the words you have learned as you read about Dracula. Write down the word or words that you think are the most important—that you would like to remember.

_____

_____

On the Trail of a Living Monster

What do you already know?

Some people believe there are real monsters that live in different parts of the world. Have you read or heard about any of these monsters? Write three things that you already know about such monsters. Work with a partner, if you like.

1. _____

2. _____

3. _____

Make predictions

Look at the pictures in the article. Then write down two things you think you will learn about as you read this article.

1. _____

2. _____

Set your purpose for reading

Write down one thing you hope to find out about living monsters as you read this article.

_____

_____

Learn important words

Study the meanings of the words below and how they are used in sentences. Knowing these words might help you as you read this article.

doubt—a feeling that something isn't real or true. *I doubt that Bigfoot is real.*

extinct—no longer alive anywhere. *Most scientists think animals like Bigfoot are extinct.*

analyze—study carefully. *I would like to analyze the footprints and find out if they belong to Bigfoot.*

KELSO, WASHINGTON. October 29, 1924—Five miners from this area have reported an odd event. A few weeks ago, they built a log cabin in the woods near their mine. Soon they saw strange footprints in the sand. The prints were made by naked feet but were much larger than any human foot.

Twice they saw a strange beast, more than seven feet tall. It looked like a "great hairy ape." The men fired rifles at it. They never found the beast, however.

A few nights later, the men were asleep in their cabin. They heard odd screams. Huge rocks were being thrown onto the cabin roof. The men feared for their lives, but they dared not leave the cabin. The attack went on till dawn. Then the miners fled.

Searchers went back to the miners' cabin. It had been wrecked. Huge rocks lay all around. Big footprints, larger than any man's, marked the ground. Yet no beast has been found.

Using skills and strategies

Reading pictures

Often you can learn more about what you read if you study the pictures carefully. The pictures add to what the words tell you.

Look at the drawings on the bottom of this page. How are the ape, human, and other creature alike? How are they different? Mark on the drawing or write in the margin the differences you notice.

BLUFF CREEK, NORTHERN CALIFORNIA. November 1, 1967—For years, there have been reports of a strange creature in this area. Hundreds of footprints have been found. Hairy beasts have been seen. Most reports say the beasts are seven to ten feet tall. They look something like apes. They have thick, dark fur and long arms. They have wide shoulders and a short neck. The head is low and

Bigfoot

Ape

Human

somewhat pointed. The beasts are not bears, nor are they apes. Apes don't walk—or run—on two legs. This beast does. People call it Bigfoot.

Last month, Roger Patterson made the first film ever of Bigfoot. Patterson is a rancher from Washington. He and a friend were camping in the woods near Bluff Creek. While riding horses, they saw a Bigfoot. It was a female.

The horses reared up. Bigfoot saw them. She began to walk away. Patterson grabbed his movie camera. He ran to follow the beast. The film in his camera was almost used up, but he had 28 feet left. On those 28 feet, he filmed Bigfoot walking through the forest.

Scientists are now studying the film. Was the creature really Bigfoot? Or was it a tall man in a monkey suit? Scientists hope to agree on an answer soon.

WALLA WALLA, WASHINGTON. September 5, 1982— Grover Krantz is one scientist who has no doubts about Bigfoot. He's sure that it is real. Krantz teaches classes at a college in Washington. Over the years, he has collected 65 plaster casts. They are all of footprints. He believes they were made by twenty different Bigfoot monsters.

The newest prints were found recently. The man who found them was not a "nut." He works for the Forest Service. He made plaster casts of the prints. Hundreds of people have done the same thing. These prints, however, were different. They were in very fine soil. Therefore, they showed many details. The casts picked up those details.

Krantz showed the casts to several fingerprint experts last week. These experts know all about fakes; they can spot one a mile away. Just to be sure, Krantz mixed a few fake casts in with the real ones. The experts could tell which

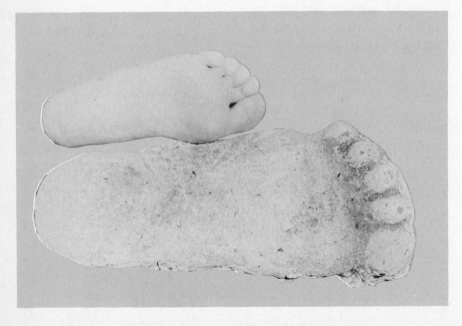

Roger Patterson compares his foot with the cast he says he made of Bigfoot.

56

Comparison of Human, Bigfoot, and Bear Prints — Left Feet

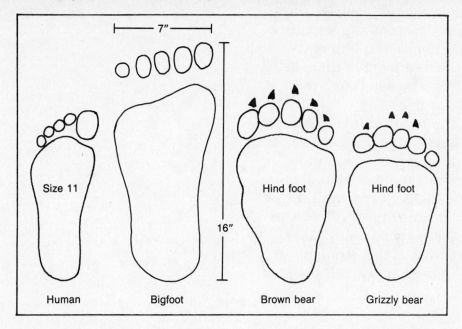

Size 11	7″ / 16″	Hind foot	Hind foot
Human	Bigfoot	Brown bear	Grizzly bear

were fakes. And the rest? All the experts believed they had come from a real animal. What kind of animal? *That* they couldn't say. It was not a known animal. Then what *was* it?

Krantz believes Bigfoot is a huge ape. He thinks it weighs eight hundred pounds. Other scientists believe such apes became extinct half a million years ago. Krantz disagrees. He thinks it still lives in the wild forests of the Northwest.

Using skills and strategies

Reading pictures

Pictures such as the one above offer you a chance to read more actively. Can you see what the scientists see in the different prints shown above? Look at the drawing carefully. How is the Bigfoot print different from a bear print? In the margin next to the drawing, write down the differences you notice.

Now look at the human footprint. How is it like a Bigfoot print? How is it different? In the margin, write what you notice.

NEW YORK. October 3, 1987—"America's favorite monster" is back in the news. Last month *Newsweek* magazine ran a long article on Bigfoot. It focused on Grover Krantz's story. Krantz has spent years studying the creature and believes there *is* a real beast out there. Still, few scientists agree.

Why not? It just doesn't make sense, say some scientists. If there *is* such a beast, there'd have to be more than one. Certainly, many people claim they've seen one. And thousands of footprints have been found. But that's very "soft" evidence. Why hasn't anyone caught a Bigfoot? Or shot one? Why haven't bones been found?

Stephen Jay Gould teaches at Harvard University. "If Bigfoot exists," he asks, "why is it that all we have are fuzzy photographs and footprints?" Several top scientists have analyzed Roger Patterson's 15-year-old film of "Bigfoot." They can't say for sure, but most of them believe the creature walked too much like a person. They think it was probably a man in an ape costume.

Other scientists look at it differently. Hundreds of people have seen strange beasts. The beasts all looked like Bigfoot. No doubt many were fakes; many were dreams. But *hundreds*? They couldn't *all* be fantasy. And what about the thousands of footprints? One Bigfoot expert put it this way: Either some of the footprints are real, or all of them are fakes. But who can believe there are so many fakes?

So the questions remain: Just what *is* this strange creature? When and where will it next appear?

Think About What You've Read

Important ideas

1. The article describes some areas where Bigfoot was seen and prints were found. What areas were these?

_____

2. This article included reports from several different places over a long period of time. How many years of Bigfoot study does it report on?

_____

_____

3. Do you believe that Bigfoot is real? Why or why not? Use statements from the article to support your opinion.

_____

_____

_____

_____

Use what you've learned before

4. Name three ways in which Bigfoot is like the monsters in myths.

_____

_____

_____

Important word meanings

Circle a sentence in the article where each word below is used. Then choose three words and write your own sentence for each word you chose.

analyze   doubt   evidence   extinct   fantasy

_____

_____

_____

_____

_____

Using skills and strategies

Look at the photo on page 56 of a human foot and a cast of a Bigfoot print. What can you find in the photo to support the idea that Bigfoot is real? Or, what do you see to make you doubt Bigfoot is real? Tell what you see.

_____

_____

_____

_____

Writing

Imagine that you're one of the people looking for Bigfoot. On a separate piece of paper, write a short letter to a friend. First, tell why you'd like to find Bigfoot. Then tell what you would do if you _did_ find Bigfoot.

Your important ideas

Look back over the article. Write down one idea that seems to be the most important one to you—the one idea that you would like to remember.

_____

_____

Your important words

Look back at the words you have learned as you read about Bigfoot. Write down the word or words that you think are most important—that you would like to remember.

_____

_____

The King of Monster Movies

What do you already know?

Do you know any tricks that movie makers use to make fantasy in movies look real? Talk about this with a partner. Then describe in a few words a trick you know of.

_____

_____

_____

Make predictions

Look at the pictures in this article and also look at the headings. Then write down three things that you think you will learn about as you read the article.

1. _____

2. _____

3. _____

Set your purpose for reading

Write down one thing you hope to find out from this article about how monster movies are made.

_____

_____

Learn important words

Study the meanings of the words below and how they are used in sentences. Knowing these words might help you as you read this article.

plot—basic story. *The plot of* King Kong *tells of a giant ape who escapes in New York City.*

miniature—smaller than the real or normal size. *The miniature model of the Empire State Building looks real.*

realistic—like the real thing. *That model of an ape was so realistic that it made me scream.*

King Kong is a giant ape. He is as tall as a five-story building. He lives on a far-off island. One day, a film crew comes to make a movie. Kong falls in love with the movie's star and kidnaps her.

The members of the film crew try to save her. Finally, they capture Kong. They decide to bring him back to New York City. There, they plan to charge money to let people see this amazing beast. They're sure to become rich!

But in New York, Kong escapes. Hunters begin trailing him. Kong grabs the woman. He carries her up the side of the Empire State Building. When he reaches the top, fighter planes shoot at him. Kong swipes at them with his paws. At last, a bullet hits him. He sets the woman gently on a ledge. Then he falls 102 stories to his death.

This is the plot of a movie called *King Kong*. It was made in 1933; it's now a classic. *King Kong* was the first monster film to use many special effects. These are the tricks that make fantasy in films look real.

Using skills and strategies

*Finding the
implied main idea*

In a story, the main ideas often are not stated. Instead, they are implied. The main ideas may simply be what happened at a given time. For example, the implied main idea of paragraph 1 in the story is what happened when King Kong and the film crew met.

Can a giant ape pose for the camera?

For *King Kong*, the first problem was making a fifty-foot ape. How did the movie makers manage it? They didn't! Instead, they built an 18-inch-high model of an ape. They started with a metal frame. Over that they put rubber and sponge. Then they covered it all with rabbit fur. It looked like a miniature ape. Its arms, legs, eyes, and mouth could even be moved.

Movie film is made up of hundreds of tiny pictures called *frames*. When you watch a movie, you see 24 frames each second.

How did the movie makers film the model ape so that it looked real when it moved? First they put it in one position. They filmed a few frames of it. Then they moved the model a tiny bit. They filmed a few more frames. They moved it again. This was *very* slow work. In a full day, they could film only 700 frames this way. When the movie was shown, it would take only 29 seconds to show 700 frames! But the "ape" seemed to move smoothly. It looked realistic. Of course, many days were spent filming all the scenes of Kong moving.

In the 1933 movie *King Kong*, much time was taken to make the ape look realistic.

A model ape climbs a model building

What about Kong climbing the Empire State Building? The film makers built a miniature model of the 102-story building. They made holes up one side. Into some holes they fitted pegs. "Kong" was wired onto the pegs. The camera was placed where it couldn't see the holes and pegs. Then 12 frames were filmed. Next the pegs were moved up a bit. "Kong" was rewired to them. Another 12 frames were shot. And so it went, all the way up. When the film was shown, people saw Kong take two steps per second. He was fast—but he looked real. And so did the Empire State Building!

In the movie, when Kong reaches the top, he is attacked by planes. For this scene, the film makers called on the U.S. Navy. They hired real planes and pilots and filmed them flying over New York City. Next they bought several model planes. The smallest were 4 inches across; the largest were 15 inches across. They hung the models on thin wires. Behind the models they hung a painting of New York City. Some of the film makers moved the models to make them seem to be flying. At the same time, others filmed the scene.

Now they had three sets of frames. They had frames of the real planes. They had frames of the model planes. And they had frames of "Kong" atop the "Empire State Building." At this point, they put together parts of these three sets. They even put some frames on top of other frames. That way, they could show King Kong and the planes at the same time.

Using skills and strategies

*Finding the
implied main idea*

Reread the last paragraph on page 63. The main idea of
the paragraph is implied. Decide what the paragraph is
about. Then write the main idea in your own words in the
margin.

Look out below!

Kong's fall from the Empire State Building posed a new
problem. They could film that normally, at 24 frames per
second. But if they *showed* the film at that speed, the fall
would last only a second or two. That wouldn't look
realistic; a fall from the real Empire State Building would
last much longer. They could show the film slowly, but that
wouldn't look smooth. So they used a new trick. They sped
up the camera. They filmed almost 200 frames per second.
(Normal speed is 24 per second.) Then they showed the film
at normal speed. It worked! Kong's fall seemed to last a
long time. It looked like a fall from 102 stories up.

King Kong was the first film that had all these special
effects. It became one of the most famous monster movies.
Chances are you've seen other monster movies. Maybe they
showed a white shark. Maybe they showed strange beings
from outer space. But the same kinds of tricks were used to
make all of them. *King Kong* broke new ground in movie
making. It was the first modern monster movie.

Think About What You've Read

Important ideas

You've read about three basic tricks the film makers used
in making *King Kong*. Now you can tell how they worked.

1. How did they show a giant ape moving in a realistic way?

_____

_____

2. How did they show Kong being attacked by planes?

_____

_____

3. How did they show Kong falling from the Empire State Building?

_____

_____

Use what you've learned before

4. List two ways in which the story of *King Kong* is like the stories you read about Bigfoot.

_____

_____

_____

Important word meanings

Fill in the blank spaces below with words or phrases.
Remember the meanings of these terms:

    synonym—a word that means the same or nearly the same
    antonym—a word that means the opposite
    definition—the meaning of a word

The first word is done for you.

1. definition of plot ___what happens in a story_____

2. synonym of miniature _____

3. antonym of realistic _____

4. definition of classic _____

Using skills and strategies

In your own words, state the implied main idea of the second-from-last paragraph of the article.

_____

_____

_____

Writing

On a separate piece of paper, make a full-page ad for the movie *King Kong*. Draw some pictures for it. Also include a sentence or two that would make people want to see the movie. If you wish, you can work with a partner.

Your important ideas

Look back over the article. Write down one idea that seems to be the most important one to you—the one idea you would like to remember.

_____

_____

_____

Your important words

Look back at the words you have learned as you read about *King Kong*. Write down the word or words that you think are most important—that you would like to remember.

_____

Reviewing What You Have Learned

Some facts and ideas you have learned

You learned many important facts and ideas as you read about monsters. A few of them are listed below. Add your own important ideas to the end of this list. You can look back at the "Your important ideas" section of each lesson to remember the ideas you wrote down.

- Through the ages, people have loved monster stories because they tell about fears that all of us have.
- *Frankenstein* was written by a teenage girl. *Dracula* was based on two other stories, one of them true.
- Some people think creatures such as Bigfoot are real, and others think such creatures are extinct.
- Film makers build models of creatures and shoot film a frame at a time to make creatures seem to move.

_____

_____

_____

_____

_____

_____

Some word meanings you have learned

Here are some of the important words you learned in the articles you read. Make sure you understand their meanings. Then add important words of your own. You can look back at the "Your important words" section of each lesson to remember the words you wrote down.

evidence—something that makes people believe a statement is true. *The evidence made me think Bigfoot is real.*

original—first. *The original* Frankenstein *is different from the movie.*

miniature—smaller than the real or normal size. *The miniature King Kong was easy to move around.*

_____

_____

_____

_____

_____

Purposes for reading

Look back at the section at the beginning of every lesson called "Set your purpose for reading." Did the articles you read help you meet your purposes? If so, explain how your purpose was met. If not, write a plan for meeting your purpose.

_____

_____

_____

Using skills and strategies

Read the paragraph below. Then underline the details that support the main idea stated in the first sentence.

Alex felt nervous as he stepped to the piano to play. He had practiced for weeks. He knew he was ready. But his hands were sweaty. He glanced at the audience. All eyes were on him. He looked down again quickly. Then he sat down at the piano. He raised his hands to the keys. His fingers were shaking.

Writing: persuasion

Imagine that a younger friend told you he or she was afraid of monsters. Think about the things you've learned about monsters in this cluster. What could you say to the friend that would make him or her feel better? Write a short letter to your friend. Use a separate sheet of paper.

Revising

Go back and read the letter to your friend. Did you use names of any of the monsters or writers mentioned in this cluster? If so, did you spell all the names correctly? Check the spelling against the names in the article. If you notice any other misspelled words, mark them, also. Then make a clean copy of your letter.

Activities

1. Talk with a friend about monsters you feared when you were younger. What made those monsters so scary?
2. Make a picture of the scariest-looking monster you can draw. Then make up a plot for a movie about it.
3. See if you can borrow a video of *King Kong*, *Frankenstein*, or *Dracula* from your library or video store. Watch the movie with a friend, if you like. See which scenes look realistic to you and which look fake. Can you figure out what tricks were used to make the movie look realistic?
4. Find a book at the library about movie making or special effects to learn more about these tricks.

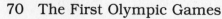 Sports

Read and learn about sports

As the runners came onto the track, the people in the stands rose. The runners were from many countries. So were the people watching. This race was the last event of the summer Olympic Games. The people from each country hoped that their athlete would win.

The runners concentrated on the race. Perhaps one of them could set a world record tonight. Sweat dripped from their faces. Then the runners lined up at the starting line. The starter raised his gun into the air. The crowd grew quiet. Each runner in the race would remember this moment for the rest of his life.

What do you already know about sports?

Talk about what you know. Get together with a group of students to talk about what you already know about sports. Here are some questions to help you get started.

1. What do you think were some of the first sports ever played?
2. Why are sports very important to some people?
3. What sports can be enjoyed by people of all ages?

Write about what you know. What is your favorite sport? Is it a sport you like to watch or play? Write a sentence that tells why it's your favorite sport.

_____

_____

_____

Make predictions

Read the titles of the articles in this cluster and look at the picture on page 69. Write down three things that you think you'll learn by reading these articles about sports.

1. _____

2. _____

3. _____

OLYMPIA-STADION BERLIN

Start to learn new word meanings

All of the words listed below are used in the two paragraphs at the top of page 68. Study the meanings of these words as you read about sports.

event—a contest in sports. *We watched every swimming event in the Sports Meet.*

athlete—a person who trains for and enjoys sports. *The athlete swims 50 laps every morning.*

concentrate—to think hard about one thing. *Basketball players need to concentrate on their shooting.*

Learn new skills and strategies

One of the strategies you will learn about in this cluster is making comparisons and contrasts. When you make a comparison, you see how two things are alike. When you make a contrast, you see how they are different. Other skills and strategies you will learn are answering questions and using sequences.

Gather new information

By the end of this cluster, you will have learned the answers to these questions.

1. Why were the first Olympic Games held?
2. What records did Babe Didrickson set?
3. What race combines swimming, biking, and running?
4. How did the light bulb make way for a new sport?
5. What is an easy sport that all of us can enjoy?

The First Olympic Games

What do you already know?

The first Olympic Games were held long ago in Greece. Write down two things that you think you know about Greece or the Olympic Games, long ago or today. Work with a partner, if you like.

1. _____

2. _____

3. _____

Make predictions

Look at the pictures in this article. Then write two things you think you will learn about as you read the article.

1. _____

2. _____

Set your purpose for reading

Write down one thing that you hope to find out about the first Olympic Games by reading this article.

_____

_____

Learn important words

Study the meanings of the words below and how they are used in sentences. Knowing these words might help you as you read this article.

athlete—one who trains for and enjoys sports. *The athlete warmed up before the race began.*

compete—to try to be better than others at doing something. *Tim competes with his brother in sports.*

event—a contest in sports. *Meg will run in the last event of the track meet.*

pentathlon—a contest made up of five different events. *Jim trained hard on all five parts of the pentathlon.*

The crowd was cheering. The runners were near the end of the race. Who would win? Suddenly, the first runner fell. The runner behind him ran past and across the finish line. The young man waved to the crowd. He had won an Olympic race. Now he was a hero. He would receive first prize. That was a ring of leaves he would wear on his head.

This race took place 3,000 years ago. However, an Olympic race was just as exciting then as now. The Olympic Games have always been something special.

Olympic honor

The first Olympics were held every four years in Olympia, Greece. People would come from all over Greece. As many as 40,000 people could watch the events. At first, however, only men were allowed to compete or watch.

At that time many Greek cities held sports events. The event at Olympia was the most important one. It was held in honor of Zeus, king of the gods. A building near Olympia held a great statue of Zeus. Athletes came there to pray to Zeus and be in the Games.

Using skills and strategies

Answering questions

Books present many facts and ideas. Questions in a book or article make sure you understand the important statements.

For example, a book may ask you this question: *When were the first Olympic Games held?* This is an important question. You need to know how long ago these events took place. The answer is 3,000 years ago.

Answer this question: *How did the Olympic Games get its name?* Write your answer in the margin above.

Changes in the games

The only event of the first 13 Olympic Games was a foot race. The runners had to run about the length of two football fields. Later, longer running races were included.

Soon boxing and wrestling were added. Another sport to be added was discus throwing. A discus is heavy and shaped like a plate. Each athlete threw it as far as he could. Still another sport added to the games was a dangerous race. In it, men raced in two-wheeled carts pulled by horses.

One event, the pentathlon, was made up of five parts. Each part tested athletes in a different sport. At the end of each part, only the best went on to the next part. First, all those competing ran a foot race. The best runners then did long jumps. Next, the athletes still in the event threw a discus. Then they threw a spear. The last two men in the event wrestled. The winner took first prize.

Using skills and strategies

Answering questions

Sometimes you read newspaper ads. You circle or underline prices or parts. This helps you remember important facts.

As you read the rest of this article, underline answers to the questions below.

1. How did a war affect the Olympic Games?
2. How did the prizes change?
3. What happened to the building where the Games took place?

Olympic wrestlers

A sculpture of an Olympic discus thrower

The end of the first Olympic Games

Rome and Greece went to war. Greece lost. Now people from Rome and other countries could compete in the Olympic Games. These athletes did not care about giving honor to Greek gods. They only cared about prizes. The prizes became bigger and worth more money. Some people cheated to win. So the king of Rome ordered the games to end. He knew that people no longer competed in the games for the joy of it.

No Olympics were held for more than 1500 years. An earthquake destroyed the building where the Olympics took place. Then the pieces were buried in a landslide. In 1875 scientists from Germany began to find pieces of the old building. This discovery gave a man in France named Pierre de Coubertin an idea. He liked the idea of people from many countries meeting together to enjoy sports. He thought it would help world peace. So he started new Olympic Games. These are the games we know today. In honor of the first Olympics, the new Olympics began in Greece.

Think About What You've Read

Important ideas

1. Where were the first Olympics held?

_____

_____

2. What was the first prize at the early Olympic Games?

_____

_____

3. Pierre de Coubertin and the king who ended the games had strong feelings about the Olympics. How were these feelings alike?

_____

_____

_____

Use what you've learned before

4. How do you think competing in the Olympic Games compares to taking part in Outward Bound?

_____

_____

_____

Important word meanings

Use a word from the list below to complete each sentence.

compete   event   Olympics   pentathlon

1. The _____ were named for the place where they were held.

2. Rome sent athletes to _____ in the Games.

3. Running and long jumping were parts of the _____

4. The last _____ is a relay race.

Using skills and strategies

Three of the questions below can be answered by reading "The First Olympic Games." Answer those three questions. Draw a line through the two questions that the article doesn't answer.

1. When did the first Olympic Games take place? _____

2. What is a discus? _____

3. What was the name of the king who stopped the first Olympics? _____

4. What was the name of the man who started today's Olympics? _____

5. What is a pentagon? _____

Writing

Imagine that there were newspapers at the time of the first Olympic Games. You are a sports reporter for the "Olympia News." On another sheet of paper, write a story about the race that took place. Tell about the runners and the people who were watching. Use details so readers can picture the event in their minds.

Your important ideas

Look back over the article. Write down one idea that seems to be the most important one to you—the one idea that you would like to remember.

_____

_____

Your important words

Look back at the words you have learned as you read about the Olympics. Write down the word or words you think are most important—that you would like to remember.

_____

_____

The Most Amazing Sports Records

What do you already know?

Who are some people who have done special things in sports? Write three facts that you already know about them. Work with a partner, if you like.

1. _____

2. _____

3. _____

Make predictions

Look at the pictures in the article and read the headings in large type. Then write down three things that you think you will learn about by reading "The Most Amazing Sports Records."

1. _____

2. _____

3. _____

Set your purpose for reading

Write down one or two things that you hope to learn about records that people have set in sports.

_____

_____

Learn important words

Study the meanings of the words below and how they are used in sentences. Knowing these words might help you as you read this article.

amazing—hard to believe. *It was amazing that the player made the basket.*

feat—a great action or deed. *Jim was known for his feat of winning three events.*

record—a list of important "best" facts. *Do you know what the record is for the most home runs in a year?*

Picture yourself in a race car on a track. You pass the lead car. You're near the record for speed. You might set a new record! Your heart pounds. What a feeling! You're the first person ever to go this fast!

Other sports may not be as exciting as car racing. In each one, however, someone has set an amazing record. And someone else is trying hard to break that record.

Using skills and strategies

Comparison and contrast

You compare things when you see how they are alike. For example, you might compare your favorite movies. Perhaps they are alike because they are all adventures.

The records in the next three paragraphs are alike. They were both set by chance.

Records set by chance

Some records just happen. A lucky golf stroke or just being in the right place at the right time can put a person in the record books.

Golf is a game for all ages. On January 13, 1985, 99-year-old Otto Bucher proved this fact. He is the oldest person ever to make a hole-in-one.

The next record is no fish story. Alf Dean caught a great white shark. The shark weighed 2,664 pounds. It was over 16 feet long. Alf set his record on April 21, 1959.

Records set on purpose

Some records are set by chance. Other records are set on purpose. People choose to do unusual feats. Do you want to enter the record books? Here are some hints. Have someone watch you set the record. Also, choose your feat carefully. Make sure that no one else has done it. Find out the best that anyone has done in a particular event. Then train until you can do better.

Would you like to set a record by lifting weights? Practice lifting an elephant over your head. In a way that is what Paul Anderson did on June 12, 1957. He lifted the greatest weight ever raised: 6,270 pounds. He didn't lift the weight over his head, however. He just lifted it off the ground.

Do you think 100 jumping jacks might set a record? Think again. August John Hoffman, Jr., did 40,014 jumping jacks in 24 hours without stopping.

Can you walk to a record? George Meegan did. He walked 19,017 miles. George went from the southern tip of South America all the way to Alaska. The walk took him 2,426 days. That is more than 6½ years.

The Most Amazing Sports Records

John Hoffman did over 40,000 jumping jacks in 24 hours.

Maybe you'll set a record in climbing rope. For that feat, you must use only your hands. In 1947, Garvin Smith needed only 4.7 seconds to climb 25 feet. That's the height of a 2-story house!

Using skills and strategies

Comparison and contrast

You contrast things when you see how they are different. Try to contrast ideas in your reading. This helps you see where the writer is going. Each new idea leads toward the point the writer is making.

The section you just read told you more about sports records. How are these records different from the first group of records? Write your answer in the margin.

Famous record holders

Some people don't stop at doing one amazing thing. Babe Didrikson and Jim Thorpe are two of these famous record holders.

Mildred "Babe" Didrikson was one of the greatest women athletes of all time. She didn't do well in just one sport. She did well in many! She played basketball for two years. Then she set world records in the 1932 Olympic Games. She won two gold medals in track and field events. She trained as a boxer. She played baseball, football, and tennis. She became a fine swimmer. Babe is best known as a golfer. She won 17 important golf matches in a row. The newspapers named her the best woman athlete of the first half of the 1900s.

Babe Didrikson

Jim Thorpe

Jim Thorpe was once described as the greatest athlete in the world. He earned honors in high school for playing football. Then he went on to the 1912 Olympics. There he won two gold medals in track and field events. One of those events was the decathlon. That event has ten parts. Jim was best in almost all of them. Then Jim played baseball and football on major league teams. His ability and fame helped to make football well liked. Before he died, Jim Thorpe was voted into the Football Hall of Fame.

Do you want more information about amazing sports records? Read the *Guinness Book of World Records*. Who knows? Maybe someday your name will be in the book!

Using skills and strategies

Comparison and contrast

Reread "Famous record holders" about the two famous athletes. Look for ways their lives are the same. Look for ways they are different. In the space above, write the words *Same* and *Different*. Under these headings write details from the paragraphs.

Think About What You've Read

Important ideas

1. What athlete won 17 golf matches in a row?

_____

2. Why must someone watch when you try to set a new record?

_____

3. Why do you think people are always trying to set new records in sports?

_____

_____

Use what you've learned before

4. Imagine you could set a record in a sports event. Why would you like to set this new record at the Olympic Games?

_____

_____

_____

Important word meanings

Fill in each blank in the sentences with one of the words below. Then write your own sentence using each vocabulary word.

amazing   athlete   feat   pentathlon   record

1. Spencer gets attention with his _____ of running backwards.

_____

2. Isn't it _____ that one person can do well in so many different sports?

_____

3. The athletes didn't rest until the five parts of the

_____ were over.

_____

4. At fifteen, Joe Nuxhall set the _____ for being the youngest major league baseball player.

_____

5. The _____ trained hard to get in shape.

_____

Using skills and strategies

A chart is one way of showing comparisons and contrasts. Most charts have headings at the top or side to tell you what each row or column is about. Use the information from the article to fill in the spaces on the following chart.

Sport	Name	Sports Record	Date or Time
Weightlifting		greatest weight ever lifted by a human	
	Otto Bucher		
		caught the largest fish	
Walking			2,426 days

Writing

You have just broken a new world record! Write a letter to your mother, father, or another adult. Tell what your amazing record is, how you did it, and how you feel about yourself. Write your letter on a separate sheet of paper.

Your important ideas

Look back over the article. Write down one idea that seems to be the most important to you—the one idea that you would like to remember.

_____

_____

_____

Your important words

Look back at the words you have learned as you read about sports records. Write down the word or words that you think are most important—that you would like to remember.

_____

_____

Racing in the Ironman Triathlon

What do you already know?

A triathlon includes swimming, running, and riding a bicycle in the same race. Write down three facts that you already know about triathlons. Work with a partner, if you like.

1. _____

2. _____

3. _____

Make predictions

Look at the pictures on pages 83 and 84. Next skim the article. That is, look through the article for ideas that are easy to notice. Then write down two things that you think you will learn about as you read the article.

1. _____

2. _____

Set your purpose for reading

Write down one thing that you really hope to find out about the Ironman Triathlon as you read this article.

_____

_____

Learn important words

Study the meanings of the words below and how they are used in sentences. Knowing these words might help you as you read this article.

train—to prepare for a sport by practice. *Lifting weights helped Susan train for her swim.*

concentrate—to think a great deal about one thing and nothing else. *Athletes must concentrate on their sport events.*

dehydration—a large loss of water from the body. *The heat caused the runner to have dehydration.*

Tim and I stepped off the plane. We felt like we had walked into an oven. My first thought was, "How am I going to race in this heat?" I could tell that my brother felt the same way.

Tim said, "Bob, we can't turn back now. We're here in Hawaii to become 'Ironmen.' Let's do it!"

Using skills and strategies

Sequence

The way in which you do things is often important. For example, you don't put on your shoes before your socks.

Listed below are the main ideas of the next four paragraphs. The ideas are out of order. Read the paragraphs to find the main ideas. In the margin, write the letters of the main ideas in the correct order, or sequence.

A. Preparing for the race   C. Changing our minds

B. Finding out about the race   D. The parts of the race

Finding out about the Ironman Triathlon

Tim and I first learned about the "Ironman Triathlon" from reading about it. The race is also shown on TV.

The triathlon has three events. First, there is a 2.4-mile swim. Then, without a stop, there is a 112-mile bike race. Last, the racers must run 26.2 miles. From start to finish the race must be finished in less than seventeen hours. I was amazed to learn that the record for the Ironman is less than half that time!

Tim thought that the athletes must be crazy to put themselves through the tough race. But the more we learned about this race, the more interested we got. We both felt that we could get into shape. After all the work, just finishing the Ironman Triathlon would be a great honor.

We decided to train for the race. Before we started training, we bought things we would need for the race. These included a racing bike, running shoes, and a swimsuit for each of us. It cost us around $800.00 just to get started.

Using skills and strategies

Sequence

Many articles have words that give clues about the sequence, or order, of events. Clue words can include *first*, *then*, *next*, and *last*. Phrases like *just then*, *later on*, and *in the morning* also tell you sequence. As you read the rest of this article, circle all the clue words you find.

The brothers trained on bikes two hours every morning.

Training for the Ironman Triathlon

Tim was a better swimmer than I was. But I could run longer than Tim. These differences helped us train. When one of us would start to tire, the other one would shout, "Keep going!"

We tried to follow a plan in our training. First, from 7:00 A.M. to 9:00 A.M., we would ride bikes. Then, around noon, we would swim for an hour and a half. Next, 5:30 P.M. to 6:30 P.M., was our time to run seven miles. We would lift weights for about forty minutes later in the evening. Some days we would concentrate on our poor events, mine being swimming.

Race day

Over two hundred athletes lined up in the early morning, ready to swim. Tim and I shook hands. We wished each other luck. Then the sound of the gun started the swim. I began to feel tired toward the end of the swim. Tim was ahead of me and already out of the water. All I could concentrate on was that I had only 138 miles to go!

The bike ride was next. I pulled on shoes, socks, and shorts and got on my bike. By now many racers were drinking lots of water. It was hot. The sun could cause dehydration. Your body can lose two to six pints of water an hour racing in this weather. I received an orange, a banana, juice, and lots of kind words at stations along the way. I kept drinking water because I knew that dehydration could make me sick.

My legs were sore by early afternoon. But Tim had slowed down and I was about to pass him. Suddenly his bike tire went flat. We were in this together, so I helped him put in a new tire tube.

By evening, the winner of the triathlon had finished and gone home. Tim and I still had twenty miles to run. Dehydration had not set in. But the pain in my legs made me walk instead of run.

I saw the finish line sixteen hours after I began. Just then, my legs stopped working. I didn't think I could walk anymore. The only way I could finish would be to crawl. Then Tim came up behind me and shouted, "You can do it! Go for it!"

I really had to concentrate to stay on my feet. Finally, I heard the cheering crowd. My brother and I became "Ironmen."

Think About What You've Read

Important ideas

1. What three events make up the Ironman Triathlon?

_____

2. How did the weather affect the race?

_____

3. How did having both brothers race together help them finish the race?

_____

Use what you've learned before

4. How are the athletes in the Olympics and the Ironman Triathlon alike?

_____

_____

Important word meanings

Each word in dark type is followed by two pairs of words with different meanings. Circle the word in each pair that gives a clue about the meaning of the word in dark type.

1. **concentrate**   think or sing   a lot or a little

2. **dehydration**   height or water   loss or gain

3. **train**   work or rest   before or after

4. **record**   true or false   lies or facts

5. **pentathlon**   three or five   events or buildings

6. **athlete**   animals or sports   interested or bored

Using skills and strategies

Tell the sequence of these events. Number them from 1 to 6. Use the clue words to help you remember the sequence.

____ **A.** After the swimming, I had only 138 miles to go!

____ **B.** By evening, I could run no more.

____ **C.** In the early afternoon, Tim's tire went flat.

____ **D.** Before I got on my bike, I put on special clothes.

____ **E.** Finally we became "Ironmen."

____ **F.** First came the morning swim.

Writing

Think of a new kind of triathlon. Describe the three events of your race in a newspaper ad. Write your ad on a separate sheet. Give your triathlon a name.

Your important ideas

Look back over the article. Write down one idea that seems to be the most important one to you—the one idea that you would like to remember.

_____

_____

Your important words

Look back at the words you have learned as you read about the Ironman Triathlon. Write down the word or words that you think are most important—that you would like to remember.

_____

_____

_____

A Winning Team: Edison and Naismith

What do you already know?

Some sports are only played outdoors. Others are played indoors. Write down three athletic events that are played indoors. Work with a partner, if you like.

1. _____

2. _____

3. _____

Make predictions

Look at the pictures in the article. Then write three things that you think you will learn about as you read this article.

1. _____

2. _____

3. _____

Set your purpose for reading

Write down one thing you hope to find out about the sport of basketball as you read this article.

_____

_____

Learn important words

Study the meanings of the words below and how they are used in sentences. Knowing these words might help you as you read this article.

experiment—test done to try out an idea. *Edison's experiment with electric light worked.*

invention—something thought up for the first time. *After the invention of the light bulb, people could play sports at night.*

responsible—to be the cause for. *Naismith is responsible for the game of basketball.*

Can one invention change the world of sports? The invention of the light bulb did just that. Before the light bulb, people could not see well indoors. They had only candles and fires. Almost all sports were played outdoors. Most of these games couldn't be played in the winter.

Thomas Edison and James Naismith changed that. Edison gave the world a source of indoor light. Naismith gave the world its most popular indoor game.

Using skills and strategies

Making predictions

You're at a book rack. You look through many books. How do you choose one? You use what you see to make predictions, or think ahead. You guess what is inside.

You can make predictions about what is in this article. Think about what you've read so far. Look at the pictures. Read the headings. Then predict what you will learn. Write your prediction in the margin. Circle your prediction if it's the same as the prediction you made on page 86.

Thomas Edison's great invention

Thomas Edison wondered about how things work. He was always asking questions. He asked "Why?" He asked "Why not?" He did many experiments to find answers. Sometimes he would work for many days and stop only for naps.

Thomas Edison's experiments had wonderful results. He was responsible for inventions like the phonograph and movie camera. He set up the first movie studio.

One of Edison's ideas was to make small lights for people to use in their homes. At that time no one knew much about electricity. Scientists were doing experiments to learn about it. Edison was sure he could use it to power house lights. He decided to invent a light bulb. It would glow when electricity passed through a wire inside the bulb.

Edison and his helpers spent nearly two years doing experiments. They could not find the right kind of thin wire for the light bulb. Then one day Edison took a piece of sewing thread and baked it. He placed it in a bulb. Much to his surprise, it worked! The thread glowed when electricity passed through it. In October of 1879 this first light bulb glowed for almost two days straight.

James Naismith's great idea

Edison's light bulb opened the door for indoor sports. People were looking for good games they could play inside in the winter. At first, they tried to play games like soccer. This didn't work. People got hurt and windows were broken.

This picture was taken in 1900, nine years after the first game was played.

Using skills and strategies

Making predictions

In the section you just read, you learned that people were looking for a new indoor sport. What do you think the rest of the section will tell you? Write your prediction in the margin. Finish the article to see if your prediction is right.

James Naismith was a gym teacher in Springfield, Massachusetts. The time was December 1891. Naismith's students were bored. They wanted a new, active indoor sport. So the teacher made himself responsible for coming up with a game. He chose to use a soccer ball in his game. It was big and easy to catch. Then he asked a worker for two large boxes. He planned to use the boxes as goals. Instead, the worker gave him two peach baskets. Naismith tied the baskets to high railings on either side of the gym.

Naismith described the rules of the game to his gym class. The students played the first game in December 1891. The boys loved the game and taught it to friends in other schools.

It didn't take long for this sport to catch on. Many high school and college teams started playing it. People first wanted to call this new game Naismith Ball. But we know it today as basketball. Edison's invention made possible a great game now played by millions!

Think About What You've Read

Important ideas

1. Why did James Naismith invent the game of basketball?

_____

_____

2. Why is the light bulb important for indoor basketball?

_____

_____

Use what you've learned before

3. What other sports are played indoors or at night because of the light bulb?

_____

_____

Important word meanings

In the article, underline a sentence where these words are used: *experiments*, *invention*, *responsible*. Then write a sentence for each word on a separate sheet of paper.

Using skills and strategies

Look back at the two predictions you made before reading the article. Tell why you made one of these predictions. Use a separate sheet of paper.

Writing

Imagine you keep a diary. Every day you write about things you do. Today you played basketball for the first time in Mr. Naismith's gym class. Describe on a separate sheet any funny events that took place during that game.

Your important ideas

Look back over the article. Write down one idea that seems to be the most important one to you—the one idea that you would like to remember.

_____

Your important words

Look back at the words you learned as you read the article. Write down the word or words that you think are most important—that you would like to remember.

_____

Ten Sports for a Lifetime

What do you already know?
Some sports can be enjoyed by people for a lifetime. Write three facts that you know about such sports. Work with a partner, if you like.

1. _____

2. _____

3. _____

Make predictions
Look at the pictures and read the headings in large type in the article. Then write down two things that you think you will learn about by reading "Ten Sports for a Lifetime."

1. _____

2. _____

Set your purpose for reading
Think about how active you have been in sports until now. Then write down one thing you want to learn about sports by reading this article.

Learn important words
Study the meanings of the words below and how they are used in sentences. Knowing these words might help you as you read this article.

exercise—to move the body in order to become more fit. *The athlete needs to exercise his stiff leg.*

equipment—outfits or supplies. *We bought new camping equipment at the sports store.*

healthy—well. *Eating the right foods helps you stay healthy.*

muscles—body fibers that shorten and lengthen to help a body move. *The woman lifted weights to strengthen her arm muscles.*

Name one thing that your whole family can do together. It makes you use your mind and your muscles at the same time. The answer is sports.

Being active in sports is important for everyone, young or old. Taking part in sports is good exercise. It can help you stay healthy for a long time. However, not all sports can be enjoyed by everyone.

Using skills and strategies

Sequence

You've learned about time sequence. It is the order in which things happen. Another kind of sequence is logical sequence. This is any order that makes sense. For example, you might want to describe your school. First, you might describe the outside of the school. Then you might tell about the inside of the school. A friend of yours might tell about the inside of the school first. Then he would describe the outside.

This article uses logical sequence. The two paragraphs you just read tell what the topic is. The rest of the article is in two parts. Circle the headings. They tell in what order the writer will explain the topic. First, the writer will tell about sports that a person can do alone. Then, the writer will tell about sports for more than one person.

Sports for one person

Walking is probably the easiest way to exercise. The only equipment you need is a comfortable pair of shoes. You get as much exercise from walking as from running. Yet there is less chance you will get hurt. The best thing about walking is that it is so natural. It doesn't seem like exercising. You can even get a healthy workout when you walk and talk with a friend. Even in very hot or very cold weather, some older people walk every day. They walk in indoor shopping malls.

Swimming works on many parts of your body at the same time. This sport uses muscles in your arms and legs. At the same time it makes your heart stronger. Think about running on a track and running in water. It is harder to move in the water. This means our bodies work harder there. Swimming programs start with babies only six weeks old. Marie Wilcox, age 65, has been swimming since she was three. She is still a strong competitor in races. She has won over 400 medals.

Biking gives you exercise and can also get you somewhere. Riding a bicycle makes your leg muscles strong. Also, it builds up the muscles in your heart. You can choose among many kinds of bikes. Your choice depends on what you want the bike for. New bikes cost from $50 to over $1,000. The first bike did not have brakes or pedals. That was about 200 years ago. Now bikes come in all shapes and sizes for all different ages.

Do you like beautiful weather and green grass? Then you might like to try golf. This sport has been around for about 800 years. To play golf, you use a thin club and a small ball. You hit the ball into a hole in the ground far from the starting point. You try to use the fewest strokes possible. You can play nine holes or eighteen holes. If several people play together, the player with the lowest score wins. Golf is good exercise even for watchers. To watch, you must walk from hole to hole. More people play golf than any other outdoor sport.

Feel the cold wind on your face as you move up the mountain. But look out coming down! You are skiing on snow. And you are moving fast. Before you ski, you must prepare. You should take lessons for your own safety. At the slopes, warm up your muscles before you start. This sport calls for a lot of special equipment. You need skis, boots, and poles. You also need something warm to wear. Skiing on snow, at your own pace, is exciting.

If you prefer the indoors, try bowling. Over 64 million Americans bowl every year. One reason is that learning to bowl is easy. There are ten pins set up at the end of a long lane. The bowler tries to roll a ball into the pins to knock them down.

The headings show that the writer put sports into two groups. You just read about sports for one person. Next you will read about sports for more than one person. As you read this section, look for the order in which the writer tells about these sports. Some of the sports require teams. Others do not. In the margin, write which sports the writer talks about first—team sports or sports that don't need teams.

Sports for more than one person

Softball is a popular team sport that is much like baseball. Over 30 million people play softball every year. The field for softball is smaller than baseball. Softball players wear less equipment than baseball players. The reason for both differences is the size of the ball. A softball is bigger than a baseball. At many family picnics both children and adults have a good time playing this sport.

"Look out! Here comes a spike!" You are likely to hear a volleyball player shouting this out. Volleyball teams take turns hitting a volleyball across a high net. Players may only use their hands. To play well, you must guess where the ball will fall. Then you must get it back over the net. Play can be a real challenge. In volleyball, you don't move around a lot. Still the sport keeps you on your toes.

Playing tennis is great exercise, indoors or outdoors. One or two players stand on each side of the court. Each player has a racket. They use their rackets to hit a ball back and forth over a net. The goal is to hit the ball where the player or players on the other side can't reach. Tennis is fun to watch. But then the only part of your body that gets exercise is your neck.

Racquetball is an indoor sport that calls for a smaller racket. This is a fast-moving game. It is played in a small room with high walls. Players bounce the ball off the walls. They try to have the ball bounce away from each other. You score points if the ball bounces on the floor twice before the other player returns the ball. Wearing glasses to protect your eyes is an important safety step for this game.

When you want exercise, try one of the sports listed in this article. Remember to start slowly and build yourself up. Eating right and exercising helps you stay healthy for a lifetime.

Think About What You've Read

Important ideas
1. Name two sports from the article that use rackets.

_____

2. Why is it harder to exercise in the water than on land?

_____

3. How would your neck get exercise by watching people play tennis?

_____

Use what you've learned before
4. After reading this article, why do you suppose the three sports in the Ironman Triathlon interest so many people?

_____

_____

_____

Important word meanings
Write the letter for each vocabulary word next to its meaning below. Then write a sentence using each word.

A. healthy   B. equipment   C. experiment
D. muscles   E. exercise   F. invention

1. _____ something thought up for the first time

_____

2. _____ body fibers that shorten and lengthen

_____

3. ____ outfits or supplies

_____

4. ____ well

_____

5. ____ a test done to try out an idea

_____

6. ____ to move in order to become more fit

_____

Skills and strategies

Look at the list below. It names the sports you might have thought about as you read the articles in this cluster.

archery	auto racing	baseball	basketball
biking	bowling	boxing	discus
diving	fishing	football	golf
gymnastics	hockey	racquetball	skating
skiing	soccer	softball	swimming
tennis	running	walking	wrestling

On a separate sheet of paper, write the headings _Sports for one person_ and _Sports for more than one person_. Write each sport in the list under the correct heading.

Writing

You and someone else in your family want to exercise every day. On a separate sheet, make a plan for what you want to do. List the days of the week and what you will do each day. Then explain how your exercise plan will help both you and the other person. Write one or two paragraphs of explanation.

Your important ideas

Look back over the article. Write down one idea that seems to be the most important one to you—the one idea that you would like to remember.

_____

_____

Your important words

Look back at the words you have learned as you read about lifelong sports. Write down the word or words that you think are most important—that you would like to remember.

_____

_____

Reviewing What You Have Learned

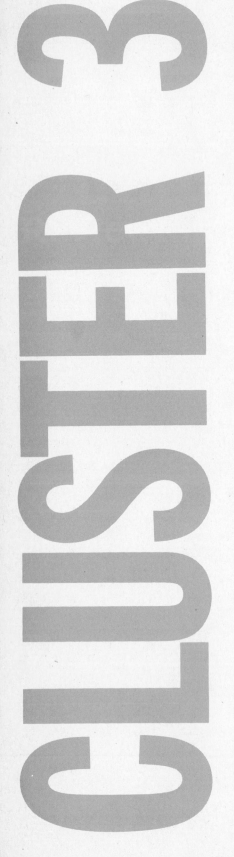

Some facts and ideas you have learned

You learned many important facts and ideas as you read about sports. A few of them are listed below. Add your own important ideas to the end of this list. You can look back at the "Your important ideas" section of each lesson to remember the ideas you wrote down.

- The first Olympic Games were held to honor Zeus.
- Babe Didrickson was one of the greatest women athletes of all time.
- A triathlon combines swimming, biking, and running.
- The invention of the light bulb let people play indoor sports like basketball.
- Walking is an easy and safe way to get exercise.

_____

_____

_____

_____

Some word meanings you have learned

Here are some of the important words you learned in the articles you read. Make sure you understand their meanings. Then add important words of your own. You can look back at the "Your important words" section of each lesson to remember the words you wrote down.

compete—to try to be better than others at doing something. _John and Al compete in handball._

dehydration—a large loss of water from the body. _You should drink water to avoid dehydration._

invention—something thought up for the first time. _Edison's invention changed the sports we play._

_____

_____

Purposes for reading

Look back at the section at the beginning of every lesson called "Set your purpose for reading." What purposes did you set for reading the articles in this cluster? Write down a purpose you set for reading that you want to remember. Did you meet that purpose? If you didn't, you might want to go to the library to do more reading.

_____

_____

Using skills and strategies

Write answers to the questions below. Look back at the articles to help you get ideas.

1. How are the Olympic Games and the Ironman Triathlon alike? How are they different?

_____

_____

2. How are the sports of bowling and tennis alike? How are they different?

_____

_____

3. How were James Naismith and Thomas Edison alike? How were they different?

_____

_____

Writing: creative thinking

Just as the light bulb changed indoor sports, other inventions could change the sports of the future. How might space travel change the way people exercise? Will future Olympics have teams from different planets?

Write one or more paragraphs describing a new event in the Olympics of the year 2292. Tell on which planet the games are being held. Tell what the athletes wear, use, and do in the event. Use a separate sheet of paper.

Revising

To a friend, read what you have written about the future Olympic Games. Does your friend have a question about your description? Can you change your description to answer the question? If so, mark your changes on your paper. Then make a clean copy of your description.

Activities

1. Listen to a sports event on the radio. Write down any interesting words that the speaker uses to describe the action. Share these words with the class. Have them try to guess what sport you were listening to.
2. Athletes do special exercises to get their bodies ready for the sport they take part in. Go to the library to find fitness books about a sport you like. Find at least three warm-up exercises that are especially good for your sport. Show these exercises to the class and tell how each exercise helps your body. Encourage your classmates to do them.

Jobs

Read and learn about jobs

People's ideas about work and jobs have changed over the years. About 3,000 years ago, people worked for one reason—to survive. Work was hard. People did what they had to do to meet their needs. About 500 years ago, people in the West began to see work as more than a way to survive. People worked to serve God, their country, and their families. Then, about 200 years ago, a new idea about work arose. This idea was that people should enjoy the work they do.

When people think about jobs today, they still work to survive. They still work to help others. But they look for more. They want a career that they will enjoy. People can choose among thousands of different careers. For example, a person can be a salesperson, reporter, or technician. They can choose almost any career they want.

What do you already know about jobs?

Talk about what you know.   Get together with a group of students to talk about what you already know about jobs. Here are some questions to help you get started:
1. Why do people have to work?
2. What are the most dangerous jobs?
3. What kinds of jobs do you enjoy most?
Write about what you know.   Write down a job you would like to have. Then write a sentence telling why you think you would like that job.

_____

_____

Make predictions

Read the titles of the articles in this cluster and look at the picture on page 99. Write down three things that you think you'll learn by reading these articles about jobs.

1._____

2._____

3._____

Start to learn new word meanings

The words listed below are used in the paragraph at the top of page 98. Study the meanings of these words as you read about jobs.

technician—a person who knows how a certain machine works. *A television technician knows how to fix TVs.*

reporter—a person who gathers news and writes or tells it to others. *The reporter wrote a story about a new factory.*

Learn new skills and strategies

You often come across new ideas as you read. One way to help make sense of these new ideas is to use information you already know. In this cluster, you will learn some ways to use what you already know. You also will learn how to use the sequence of events to help you understand what you read.

Gather new information

By the end of this cluster, you will have learned the answers to these questions.

1. How do people who have different jobs share what they know?
2. How did a fire fighter put out the biggest natural gas fire in the world?
3. What jobs could a person have on a newspaper?
4. What does a technician do?
5. What is the work tool of the future?

The Farmer and the Writer

What do you already know?
   Write down one fact you know about the work a farmer
or a writer does. Work with a partner, if you like.

_____

_____

_____

Make predictions
   Look at the pictures of the farmer and the writer. Then
write down one thing you think you will learn about each of
them.

_____

_____

_____

Set your purpose for reading
   Write down one thing you hope to find out about jobs as
you read this story.

_____

_____

Learn important words
   Study the meanings of the words below and how they are
used in sentences. Knowing these words might help you as
you read this article.

tend—to take care of. *Some farmers tend animals such as
   cows or chickens.*

bore—to tire from the same thing over again or something
   dull. *Jobs bore me if I have to work alone.*

create—to make something new. *Some writers create funny
   stories.*

There was once a land where everybody had the same job. They grew food. Some people were better than others at their job. Some people liked their job more than others.

One man in this land was a wonderful farmer. He loved his work. He treated all his plants like tiny children. He tended them day by day, watching them grow. The man grew every kind of fruit and vegetable. He ate some of the food right away. He put other food in a dark, cool place. He ate this food during the long winter.

This farmer filled the spaces around his tiny house with flowers. He picked some of them and put them all over his house. He hung some of the flowers upside down to dry. Then he filled his sleeping sack with the dried flowers. In the winter, the sweet smell of the flowers reminded him of the warm summer.

The farmer planted and grew more fruits and vegetables than he could eat. He picked more flowers than he could use. It made him sad that such beautiful things were never used. But he couldn't give up the joy of tending his garden. During the winter, the farmer was bored. He sat and waited for the cold weather to end. He wished that he had something to do.

In the same place, there was another man. He grew food, too. But this man didn't like farming. He knew little about planting and saving food. He liked writing stories. His head was filled with ideas for stories. His house was filled with the stories he had created over the years.

This man tried to grow what he needed, but it was hard for him. Instead of tending his plants, he sat outside thinking up ideas for new stories. Instead of picking the ripe fruits and vegetables, he created pictures to go along with his stories.

The little food he grew ran out long before the winter was over. Then he was too hungry to think, write, or draw. Each winter he wished he had been more of a farmer than a writer.

The two men met on the road one day. Each one talked about what he did best. They both decided that they could help each other.

What do you think they decided to do? Write an ending for the story on a separate piece of paper.

Using skills and strategies

Thinking about what you already know

Thinking about what you already know will help you write an ending for this story. You already know that a good solution for a problem is for people to cooperate. You learned that the first man in the story loves to grow things but is bored and unhappy during the winter. You also learned that the second man spends all his time thinking up stories. He has nothing to eat during the winter.

How can the the two men solve their problems? The answer to this question will help you write an ending to the story.

Think About What You've Read

Important ideas
1. Why was the farmer so unhappy when the winter came?

2. Why was the writer so unhappy when the winter came?

3. Which sentence below tells what you think the story is mostly about? Why?
   a. Every person should take care of himself or herself.
   b. Sharing what you do best is a way to make sure people get what they need.

Use what you already know
4. Do you think the writer would grow his own food if he lived today? Why?

Important Words

Look at the underlined phrase in each of the sentences below. Then write the sentence using *bored, tended,* or *created* in place of the phrase.

1. Janet <u>watered and weeded</u> her garden.

   _____

2. David was <u>tired of doing the same thing again and again.</u>

   _____

3. Jesse <u>planned, cut out the pieces, and painted</u> a mask.

   _____

Using skills and strategies

You already know a lot about the work done by farmers and writers. On the lines below, write three things you know about each of these jobs.

_____

_____

_____

_____

_____

Writing

Think about a special skill you have. Write about that skill on a separate sheet of paper. Tell what your skill is and how other people might find it useful. Share what you write with a classmate.

Your important ideas

Look back over the story. Write down one idea that seems to be the most important one to you—the one idea that you would like to remember.

_____

_____

Your important words

Look back at the words you have learned as you read about the farmer and the writer. Write down the word or words that you think are most important—that you would like to remember.

_____

Diary of a Fire Fighter

What do you already know?

Write down three things that you think you already know about fire fighters. Work with a partner, if you like.

1. _____

2. _____

3. _____

Make predictions

Look at the pictures in this article. Then look at the headings, which give a date and a place. Write down three facts that you think you will learn as you read the article.

1. _____

2. _____

3. _____

Set your purpose for reading

Write down one thing you hope to find out about fire fighting as you read this article.

_____

_____

Learn important words

Study the meanings of the words below and how they are used in sentences. Knowing these words might help you as you read this article.

fuel—anything that can be burned to produce useful heat or power. *Natural gas is a fuel found deep in the ground.*

dynamite—an explosive made in the form of sticks. *The fire fighters used dynamite to blow out the fire.*

oxygen—a gas in air that has no color and no smell. *A fire cannot burn without oxygen.*

Natural gas is a useful fuel. People use it to cook and to dry their clothes. Natural gas lies deep in the ground. To get the fuel out, workers drill a well and put pipes into the space where the gas is. Then a valve is put on the pipe so the gas flow can be turned on and off.

In 1961, a natural gas well caught fire. The well was in the Sahara Desert in North Africa. It was in one of the biggest natural gas fields in the world.

The fire was really a huge torch, 450 feet high. People 90 miles away saw it and heard it. The noise the burning gas made was like twelve jets taking off at once.

The company that owned the gas knew they had to hire the only man in the world who could put out the fire. That man was a Texan named Red Adair. He is the world's best and most famous fire fighter. He and his crew put out fires

no one else will go near. This story tells how Red put out the biggest fire of his life. It is told as Red might have written it.

Using skills and strategies

Sequence

Many stories are written in the order in which events took place. As you read these stories, you learn what happened first, what happened next, and so on. The order in which the events took place is called the sequence.

The sequence is very important in this story of the natural gas fire. Before you read each section, circle the date in the heading.

December 2, 1961, Houston

The owners of a gas well called. Can I put out a gas fire in North Africa? I told them sure. Then I called the people in Africa to find out just how big a job it is. It's big! They don't think anyone can get near the fire to put it out because of the terrible heat. "Oh, and don't forget," they said, "there's no water in the desert."

December 4, 1961, Houston

I know how to put out the fire. We'll use dynamite to blow it out, like all the others. The blast should push away the oxygen for a little while. The fire will go out. Then all we'll have to do is put something over the hole to stop the gas from shooting out. I've ordered a well head to cover the hole. It's ten feet across and weighs ten tons. It will be made for us and sent to North Africa.

December 6, 1961, North Africa

My crew and I arrived at the fire. What a sight! Enough gas shoots out of that hole to heat a big Texas town for a day. And there's a lot more gas to come. That baby will shoot and burn for a hundred years if we don't stop it now.

December 7, 1961, North Africa

My crew and I met with the people who work at the well. Our first job is to drill for water. We can't use water to put out the fire. But we'll need it to cool the machines and the crew. Otherwise, even with our special suits, we can't get near enough to do the job.

December 29, 1961, North Africa

We have the water we need. For the last three weeks, we have drilled and drilled. We found water one-half mile down. We brought it up and made three small lakes with it. And all the time, that fire keeps burning.

106

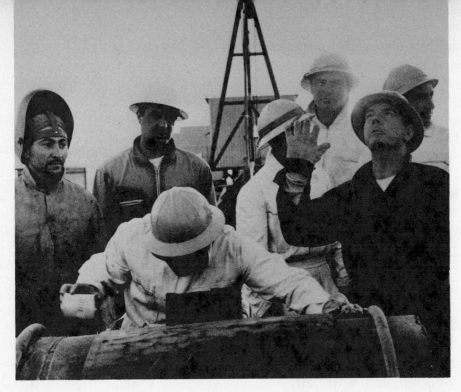

Red Adair (on the right) gives orders to his men.

Using skills and strategies

Sequence

You have learned the way that Red plans to put out the fire. You know that he plans to use dynamite to blow out the fire. Then he plans to cover the well to stop the gas leak.

As you read, look at the dates to see how long it takes Red to carry out his plan. For example, you can tell from the dates that it took Red 22 days to drill for water in the desert. How long will it take Red to put out the fire and cover the well? Write your answers in the margin.

January 5, 1962, North Africa

Happy New Year! I think we're ready to start. We built several steel huts and used bulldozers to push them near the fire. We're going to put pumps in the huts. The pumps will spray us with water when we work near the fire. Without the wall of water, we would all go up in smoke.

March 7, 1962, North Africa

Delays and more delays! It has taken a month to tend to the details. We only got the pumps a few days ago. Looks like tomorrow is it.

March 8, 1962, North Africa

Today we did it! We put out the biggest fire of my life. We tied a barrel to a bulldozer. Then we put the dynamite—500 pounds of it—inside the barrel. We laid wire from the dynamite to a hole about 100 yards away from the fire. We turned on the water. Under a wall of water, I drove the bulldozer right up to the fire.

Then I ran back to the hole and set off the dynamite. With a mighty roar and a cloud of black smoke, the dynamite went off. Then it was quiet. No more fire. No more roar of burning gas. Just hissing as the fuel shot out of the well. The fire was out, but the desert is still hot.

April 15, 1962, North Africa

I thought putting out the fire was bad! Today we stopped the gas. The well head had to be put over the hole. We couldn't use machines. A spark from a machine would have started the fire again (and probably killed us all). We worked under a wall of water. It took us three hours to put the well head on. One little spark from a tool would have been the end of us all.

May 15, 1962, Houston

Another job well done by Red Adair Oil Well Fires and Blowouts Control Company! All I have to do now is to send in my bill. I don't think they'll mind paying. After all, I stopped the biggest natural gas fire in history!

Think About What You've Read

Important ideas

1. Why did Red and his crew need to find water? How did they do it?

_____

_____

_____

2. How did Red put out the fire?

_____

_____

_____

3. Why did Red and his crew need to work under water to put the well head on even after the fire was out?

_____

_____

Use what you've learned before

4. How is Red Adair like the writer in the first story?

_____

_____

Important word meanings

Use each of the words below in a sentence. The sentence should tell something you learned in the story about Red Adair.

fuel   tend   dynamite   oxygen

_____

_____

_____

_____

Using skills and strategies

Think about what you read in the article. Read the sentences below that tell how Red put out the fire. Write _1, 2, 3,_ or _4_ in front of each one to show the order in which they happened. Look back at the article to help you.

_____ Red drove the bulldozer right up to the fire.

_____ They put 500 pounds of dynamite in the barrel.

_____ Red ran to the hole to set off the dynamite.

_____ The dynamite blew out the fire.

Writing

Pretend you were a reporter at the time the natural-gas fire first took place in the desert. Write the first paragraph of a newspaper article. Tell _what_ happened, _where_ it happened, _who_ put out the fire, and _how long_ it took to do it. Use a separate sheet of paper.

Your important ideas

Look back over the article. Write down one idea that seems to be the most important one to you—the one idea that you would like to remember.

_____

_____

Your important words

Look back at the words you have learned as you read about fire fighting. Write down the word or words that you think are most important—that you would like to remember.

_____

_____

Finding the Right Career

What do you already know?

Write down three facts you already know about finding a career. Work with a partner, if you like.

1. _____

2. _____

3. _____

Make predictions

Look at the pictures and the charts in this article. Then write down three facts that you think you will learn as you read the article.

1. _____

2. _____

3. _____

Set your purpose for reading

Write down one thing you hope to learn about finding a career as you read this article.

_____

_____

Learn important words

Study the meanings of the words below and how they are used in sentences. Knowing these words might help you as you read this article.

reporter—a person who gathers news. *The reporter asked questions about the accident.*

technician—a person who knows a lot about a certain field. *An X-ray technician knows how to use an X-ray machine.*

physical—of the body or using the body. *Working for a moving company is physical work.*

Many people would like to have Red Adair's career. The work is exciting—and probably fun. Red earns good money. His work helps people who are in trouble. How did Red become a gas- and oil-well fire fighter? When did he decide that fire fighting was the career for him? How did he prepare for his career?

Everyone who works must face these same decisions. They decide what kind of work they want to do. They learn about that work. Then they prepare themselves for that career. But how do you know what career is best for you?

Finding the Right Career

Know yourself

One way to choose a career is to pick work that you like. Look at the following list of careers. Circle three careers on the list you might like to have.

factory worker	secretary	butcher
truck driver	mechanic	builder
police officer	banker	teacher
librarian	reporter	artist
actor	clerk	nurse
technician	lawyer	doctor
cook	pilot	singer
farmer	model	writer

Using skills and strategies

Thinking about what you already know

Which three careers did you circle? One reason you probably chose them is that you already know something about them. For example, you might have chosen *technician* because you like to fix things. You might have chosen *doctor* because you think doctors earn a lot of money. Or you might have chosen *secretary* because you type well. You already know that you can do that job.

Look back at the three careers you circled. On the lines below, write one thing you know about each career. Then, name one reason why you might like to have that career. If you want to pick a career that is not on the list, do so.

_____

_____

_____

_____

_____

_____

_____

Look at the careers you chose. What do they tell about you? It's helpful to get to know yourself before you go looking for a career. You will be a better worker if you have a career that fits you.

The questions below will help you learn more about yourself. Read them and circle your answers.

1. I like to **(a)** work inside. **(b)** work outside.

2. I enjoy **(a)** working alone. **(b)** working with others.

3. I enjoy **(a)** doing the same thing each day.
   (b) doing different things each day.

4. I want to work **(a)** the same hours each day.
   (b) different hours each day.

5. I like to work with **(a)** different people each day.
   (b) the same people each day.

6. I like working with **(a)** people. **(b)** machines.

7. I'm better working with **(a)** my hands. **(b)** my head.

8. I like to **(a)** fix things. **(b)** make new things.

9. I like to **(a)** have plenty of time to think before I act.
   (b) act quickly.

10. I like **(a)** hard physical work.
    (b) work that's easy on my muscles.

There are many more questions you could ask yourself. The important thing is to decide what kind of work you like to do. Then you can use what you know about yourself to think about a career.

Get work practice

One way to choose a career is to try out different jobs now. This can help you decide what you might like to do later. Below are some jobs you might do. Think about the jobs and the questions you just answered. For each job, write down two things a person might want to know about himself or herself before taking the job.

1. Pack groceries in a grocery store.

_____

_____

2. Put away books in a library.

_____

3. Cook food and fill orders in a fast-food store.

_____

_____

There are lots of other ways to get work practice. Your neighbor may need help taking care of small children. Someone might need you to run errands. You might think of other people you could help.

When you're working, you can practice things that are important for any career you may want. For example, be on time. Do the job the way you're asked to do it. Finish the work. Do the best job you can do.

Learn about careers

Suppose you don't like to write, but you still want to work on a newspaper. Some people who work on newspapers are reporters. But there are many other careers on a newspaper. The picture shows some of the jobs that people who work for a newspaper company have. What do these people do?

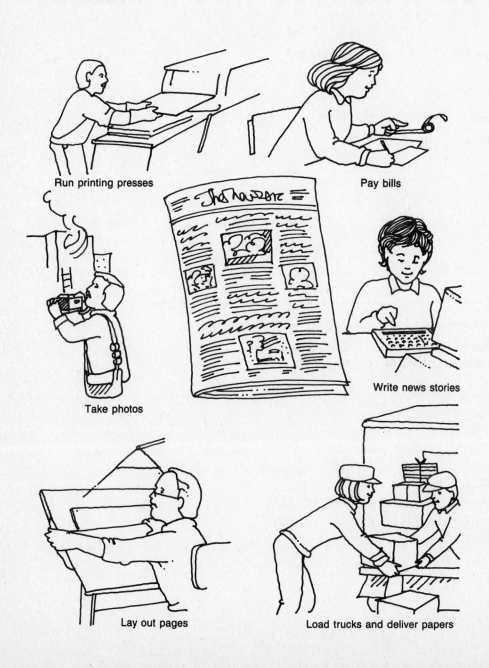

Run printing presses

Pay bills

Take photos

Write news stories

Lay out pages

Load trucks and deliver papers

As you can see, many people work for a newspaper company. This is true for other kinds of work, too. Think of a place you would like to work. Do you know how to do the kinds of work people do there?

Once you decide on a career you might want, you need to know what training you need for that career. Doctors, for example, need eight years of college. Then they need a year or two of practice before they can work as doctors. Some technicians, on the other hand, might begin their careers right out of high school. However, they need many years of on-the-job training to learn their jobs.

Think About What You've Read

Important ideas

1. Name three things you need to find the right career.

_____

_____

2. Name two reasons why people choose the careers they do.

_____

_____

3. Why do you think it is important to get a career that is right for you?

_____

_____

Use what you've learned before

4. Look at the questions on page 112. How do you think Red Adair would have answered five of them?

_____

_____

_____

Important word meanings

Find these words in the article: _technician, reporter,_ and _physical_. Circle them and write their meanings on the lines below.

_____

_____

_____

Using skills and strategies

You have to think about what you already know to answer the questions in this article. On the lines below, tell two things you know that might affect the career you choose.

_____

_____

Writing

Talk to an adult you know. Write down his or her name and what kind of career he or she has. Then ask the questions below and write down what the person says. When you are finished, tell others what you found out.

People and Careers

Name _____

Career _____

What do you do at work?

_____

_____

What do you like best about your career?

_____

What do you like least about your career?

_____

Tell me about one of your days at work.

_____

_____

Your important ideas

Look back over the article. Write down the idea that seems to be the most important one to you.

_____

_____

Your important words

Look back at the words you have learned as you read about finding a career. Write down the word or words that you think are most important.

_____

People Who Have Great Careers

What do you already know?
Write down three careers you think would be great to have. Work with a partner, if you like.

1. _____

2. _____

3. _____

Make predictions
Read the headings in the article. They tell you what four careers you will read about. Write down why you think someone might like each career.

1. _____

2. _____

3. _____

4. _____

Set your purpose for reading
Write down one thing you hope to learn as you read this article.

_____

_____

Learn important words
Study the meanings of the words below and how they are used in sentences. Knowing these words might help you as you read this article.

borrow—to get something from another person with the idea of giving it back. *Many farmers borrow money from a bank.*

design—prepare a drawing, sketch, or plan. *Bill designed a coat in class.*

equipment—what a person has or uses in a job. *A heavy bag is part of a letter carrier's equipment.*

116

Did you know there are as many careers as there are people? No matter what kind of career a person has, he or she works in his or her own way. It takes a person to make a career come alive and be more than just work. Read how some real people make their careers interesting.

Using skills and strategies

Thinking about what you already know

Think about the questions that are on page 112 as you read this article. Write in the margin how you think the people in the article would answer some of the questions. Share what you write with your classmates.

Frank and Jean—farmers

"Most people have no idea how food gets to their plate," says Jean. "They don't know where any of their food comes from. I could tell them that a lot of their food comes from farms like ours. Farmers like us grow much of the food that Americans eat."

Jean and Frank are farmers. They make money by raising and selling 2,500 pigs each year. The work is not easy, and Jean and Frank do most of it themselves.

Their day starts at five o'clock in the morning. Before breakfast, Jean and Frank are on the job. Jean starts by checking the mother and baby pigs. She takes the dirty hay out of the pen and puts in clean hay. She gives them food and water. Frank checks the older pigs. He thinks some are ready to sell.

At breakfast, Jean and Frank talk about selling the pigs. They need money to pay bills. They decide to sell 30 pigs and to borrow the rest of the money they need from the bank.

Frank enjoys his work on the farm. One of his first jobs in the morning is feeding the pigs.

By 7:30 A.M., Jean and Frank are back outside. Jean plows the corn fields until 10:30 A.M. They grow about 300 acres of corn to feed the pigs. While Jean plows, Frank picks out the pigs they will sell. He and a neighbor catch the pigs and put them on the truck. Jean will drive the pigs to a meat-packing house.

The rest of the day is spent plowing and getting the fields ready to plant. On other days, Jean and Frank fix machines or paint farm buildings. Almost all their time is spent on their farm. And that's how they like it.

Mark—movie assistant

"Next time you go to the show, stay and read all the names at the end of the movie. Maybe you'll see my name. I'm right there with many others!"

Mark is one of the many people who work together to make a movie. He helps pick the right actors and find the right place to make the movie.

"Right now, we're making a movie about a rich kid who dies and comes back to life as a poor kid. No one cares about her now that she's poor. We're trying to find one house we can use for the two main sets. We'll shoot the part about the rich kid first. Then someone can come in and redesign the house for the part about the poor kid."

People who work to make movies do not always have regular days. Sometimes they work long hours every day for a month. Then they have time off.

Mark sometimes spends hours calling people. He explains why. "Everything has to happen on time or we'll lose a lot of money. The work is exciting because I get to meet the stars. And I love to go to the movies! I hope I can learn enough to move up in the business someday. I have a great idea for a movie I'd like to make."

Using skills and strategies

Thinking about what you already know

As you read about the next two careers, think about what you know about how school can help a person have a good career. Learning math facts helps get some jobs. Being able to read and write well helps. Circle parts of the jobs that involve using numbers, reading, or writing.

Ann—clothing salesperson

"I like clothes," says Ann with a grin. "I've always loved clothes, and I always wanted a job working with clothes. In high school, I tried to design dresses. But I found I liked selling better. I think I have a good eye. I can tell what will look good on a person. When I show someone something and they like it, I feel really good."

Ann works at a small shop her uncle owns. Some days she is there alone. Then she has to add up the sales and the tax herself. This makes her nervous because she doesn't add or subtract very well. But her uncle says she will be able to get a better job if she learns how to use numbers. So Ann is now taking math classes at night.

Ann's uncle is going to help her learn how to buy the clothes for the shop. This is an important skill. Ann will be able to work for a larger store if she knows how to do this well. She might even have her own shop some day.

Tom—electronics field technician

"Every day it's something different. I never know what I will see when I walk into a place. All I know is that the plant boss is going to be on my back until I fix it."

That's what Tom says about his job as an electronics field technician. In his work, Tom fixes machines that make everything from plastic straws to potato chips. Most of the machines Tom must fix cannot be moved, so he has to go to the plant to fix them. Tom works for an electric company. He is paid well because he can fix machines quickly. This saves the plant bosses time and money.

Tom was driving to work a few weeks ago when his car phone rang. It was his boss. "Don't come to the office. Go right over to Cardboard Container Company. Their paper-folding machine is down."

There were very few cars in the parking lot when Tom arrived at the plant. He took his test equipment out of his trunk and walked in. No one knew what had gone wrong. One minute the machine was cutting and folding the huge roll of cardboard into holders for cans of pop. The next minute nothing was happening.

Tom started with the fuses. He found that the three large fuses that led to the machine were OK. He thought the problem must be in the machine itself. So he pulled off the large cover that protected the 70-foot machine. He took the controls out and tested them. They were OK, too.

Then he tested the motor, which was almost as tall as he was. There was nothing wrong there. Now he knew the problem had to be somewhere between the huge roll of cardboard and the motor. He was right. He found a loose wire.

Three hours after he had started, he put the cover back on the controls. He pressed the START button. The motor started. The ten-foot-high roll of cardboard at the end of the machine began to turn faster and faster. Cardboard cartons came out of the front of the machine. Tom looked at all the parts of the machine as it ran. It was working well.

Think About What You've Read

Important ideas

1. How do Jean and Frank get money when they need to pay bills?

_____

_____

2. Why doesn't Ann like to work at the shop by herself?

_____

_____

3. What kind of person do you think Tom is to be able to do his job so well?

_____

_____

Use what you've learned before

4. The company Tom went to makes cardboard cartons. What kinds of jobs do you think other people have at the cardboard container company?

_____

_____

Important word meanings

Choose a word from the list below to complete each sentence. Then write a sentence of your own using the word.

borrow   equipment   technician   design

1. George wants to _____ a new set for the movie.

_____

2. Fran loaded the _____ for her job on the truck.

_____

3. Sarah will _____ the money she needs from a bank.

_____

4. Stan is a _____ who fixes radios.

_____

Using skills and strategies

Use what you already know to answer these questions.

1. Name two pieces of equipment that Frank and Jean have on their farm.

_____

2. In what city do you think Mark works?

_____

3. Name two things Ann must learn to open her own store.

_____

4. What tools does Tom use in his job?

_____

Writing

What job do you think would be great? Is it a job you can only dream about (like coaching a major league team)? Or is it a job that you could really have someday (like coaching another team)? On a separate sheet of paper, write two or three sentences telling about the job. Start your first sentence this way: *If I could have any job I wanted, I'd like to . . . .*

Your important ideas

Look back over the article. Write down one idea that seems to be the most important one to you—the one idea that you would like to remember.

_____

_____

Your important words

Look back at the words you have learned as you read about careers. Write down the word or words that you think are most important—that you would like to remember.

_____

Computers in Your Future

What do you already know?

Write down three facts you already know about how people work with computers. Work with a partner, if you like.

1. _____

2. _____

3. _____

Make predictions

Look at the pictures in this article. Then write down three things you think you will learn as you read this article.

1. _____

2. _____

3. _____

Set your purpose for reading

Write down one thing you hope to find out about computers in the future as you read this article.

_____

_____

Learn important words

Study the meanings of the words below and how they are used in sentences. Knowing these words might help you as you read this article.

keyboard—the set of keys in a piano, a typewriter, or a computer. *All the letters and numbers are on a computer keyboard.*

input—coded information that is put into a computer. *Wrong input kept the computer from solving the problem.*

output—information put out by a computer. *The output is shown on a screen or typed on a printer.*

programmer—a person who uses a computer language to tell a computer what to do. *A programmer uses a computer language.*

A police officer uses one to track down a stolen car. A checker in a food store uses one to add grocery prices. A dancer uses one to make sure her legs are moving the right way. A news reporter uses one to write a story. A DJ uses one to keep track of how many times he plays a certain song. A scientist uses one to follow a snowstorm. A doctor uses one to find a disease. All these people use a computer in their work. You probably will use one in your work also.

How a computer works

A computer does not think by itself. People first have to put in words or numbers. Then the computer puts the words and numbers through a program. Only then can it give you some answers. People can do the same work that a computer does, but the computer does it much more quickly. And computers do not make mistakes—if they are given the right information.

Using skills and strategies

Thinking about what you already know

As you read the rest of this article, think about what you already know about computers. Write in the margin two of the things you have done with a computer. Have you used one to check math? Have you used one to do other schoolwork? Have you played games on one?

The parts of a computer

A computer has several parts. You can put words or numbers into the computer by typing them on a keyboard. The computer stores what you put in. That information becomes part of the computer's memory. The input is usually stored on a disk. A control unit picks the right information and uses it when you need it. You see the information you want on an output device. This might be a screen that looks like a TV, or it might be a typed piece of paper.

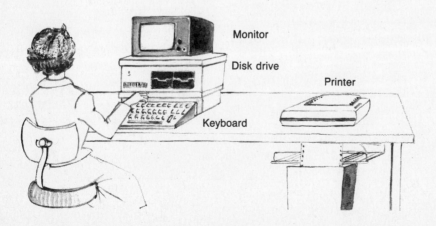

Monitor

Disk drive

Printer

Keyboard

The heart of a computer's control unit is a tiny chip. This man's job is designing and making computer chips.

Using computers at work

There are many jobs for people who know how to use computers now. And in the future, there will be even more. For example, you might learn computer languages so you could tell computers what to do. This is called programming. There will be many jobs for programmers in the years to come. Programmers can work in banking, in health, in schools, and in many different businesses.

Many people learn to use computers when they start a job. The on-the-job training shows them how to use the computer to do that job. For example, a beginning typist learns to use a computer called a word processor. A person starting out as a travel agent learns to use a computer to check flight times. A printer learns to use a computer to mix colors of ink.

Any way you look at it, computers are in your future. If you play it right, the future could be very bright.

Think About What You've Read

Important ideas

1. List four people who use computers in their work.

_____

_____

2. What are two ways to learn how to use computers for a job?

_____

_____

3. How are computers useful on the job?

_____

_____

_____

Use what you've learned before

4. Think about the people and the jobs you have read about in this cluster. Which of them might use a computer? What makes you think as you do?

_____

_____

_____

Important word meanings

Find these words in the article: _keyboard, input, programmer,_ and _output._ Circle them and write their meanings next to them in the margins. Then, on the lines below, use each word in a new sentence about how to use a computer.

_____

_____

_____

_____

Using skills and strategies

Look at the picture of the computer on page 123. Write these labels on the picture in the right places: _input, storage,_ and _output._

Writing

On a separate piece of paper, write a letter to a friend who thinks going to computer class is stupid. Tell your friend why he or she should keep going. Give reasons in your letter. Try to get your friend to see how important computers will be in the future. Share your letter with your classmates.

Your important ideas

Look back over the article. Write down one idea that seems to be the most important one to you—the one idea that you would like to remember.

_____

_____

Your important words

Look back at the words you have learned as you read about computers. Write down the word or words that you think are most important—that you would like to remember.

_____

_____

Reviewing What You Have Learned

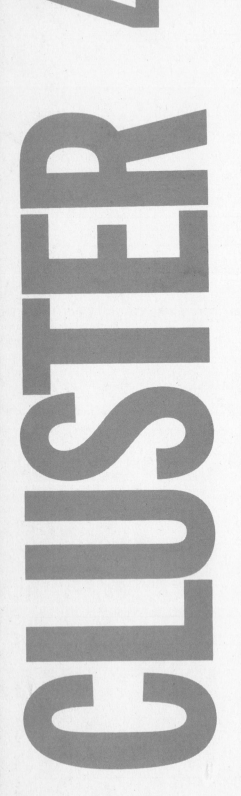

Some facts and ideas you have learned

You learned many important facts and ideas as you read about jobs. A few of them are listed below. Add your own important ideas to the end of this list. You can look back at the "Your important ideas" section of each lesson to remember the ideas you wrote down.

- People do different jobs so people don't have to do everything for themselves.
- Fire fighters use dynamite to blow out a fire.
- Knowing how you like to work will help you find work you like to do.
- Many people like the work they do.
- People use computers to do many kinds of work.

_____

_____

_____

_____

Some word meanings you have learned

Here are some of the important words you learned in the articles you read. Make sure you understand their meanings. Then add important words of your own. You can look back at the "Your important words" section of each lesson to remember the words you wrote down.

fuel—anything that can be burned to produce useful heat or power. _Natural gas is a fuel used for cooking and heating._

borrow—to get something from another person with the idea of giving it back. _Can I borrow your computer?_

physical—of the body or using the body. _Working for a moving company is physical work._

_____

_____

_____

Purposes for reading

Look back at the section at the beginning of every lesson called "Set your purpose for reading." Did you meet all of the purposes you set? If not, select one of the purposes you didn't meet. Tell what you can read to help meet that purpose.

_____

_____

Using skills and strategies

You knew a lot about jobs before you read the articles in this cluster. You talked about what you knew and you wrote down facts about each topic. Look back at the sections called "What do you already know?" to read what you wrote.

How did you use the things you already knew to understand the articles you read? On the lines below, write two things you already knew that helped you when you read the articles.

_____

_____

_____

Writing: explanation

Choose a career you think you would be good at. Then, on a separate piece of paper, write a paragraph to explain why you think you would be good at that career. Your first sentence should name the career. The rest of the paragraph should give three reasons why you want the career.

Revising

Check what you have written. Then read it to another person. Ask him or her to tell you the reasons why you picked the career you did. If the person cannot do this, make your paragraph clearer.

Activities

1. Look back at the picture on page 113 that shows the jobs at a newspaper. Make a picture like this to show the different jobs people have at your school. Work with a partner, if you like.
2. Ask your teacher to get an application form for a job from a large company. What things do companies want to know about people before hiring them? Practice filling out the form.
3. Many people may work at home in the future. They will work on computers. The computers will be connected by phone lines to a central office. Discuss the idea of working at home with some of your classmates. Talk about these questions:
   a. Would you like to work at home instead of a factory or office?
   b. Would you feel lonely working by yourself at home?
   c. Would you like a job where you wouldn't have to travel to work?
   d. What training would a person need to be able to work at home?

ACKNOWLEDGMENTS

Photo Credits

Cluster 1: 5: Jeff Rotman. **7:** Alvin Upitis/Image Bank Chicago. **8:** David Hiser/Image Bank Chicago. **11:** Earth Scenes/© W. Gregory Brown. **17:** Gamma-Liaison. **20:** Reuters/Bettmann Newsphotos. **23:** Amundsen expedition to the South Pole. A member of the expedition, Lieutenant Helmer Hanson, with team of dogs. Photograph, ca. 1911. The Bettmann Archive. **25:** The Bettmann Archive. **26:** The Bettmann Archive. **29:** ©Peter Menzel/Stock Boston. **31:** Arnaud Borrel/Gamma-Liaison. **32:** Peter Fronk/Click/Chicago.

Cluster 2: 37: ©Lucasfilm/Shooting Star. **45:** Mary Wollstonecraft Shelley (1707-1851). Head & shoulders portrait with pen in hand by Samuel John Stump. The Bettmann Archive. **47:** The Bettmann Archive. **50:** The Bettmann Archive. **51:** The Bettmann Archive. **56:** AP/Wide World Photos. **61:** The Bettmann Archive. **62:** The Bettmann Archive. **63:** The Bettmann Archive.

Cluster 3: 69: Reuters/Bettmann Newsphotos. **71:** Ancient Olympic Games: A victor in the Olympic Games entering the Temple of Zeus. Engraving, drawn by A. Castaigne. The Bettmann Archive. **72 (left):** Alinari/Art Resource, The Discus Thrower, Paris, Louvre. **72 (right):** Scala/Art Resource, The Wrestlers, Florence, Uffizzi. **78 (left):** UPI/Bettmann Newsphotos. **78 (right):** UPI/Bettmann Newsphotos. **83:** Ellis Herwig/Gartman Agency. **84:** AP/Wide World Photos. **87:** The Bettmann Archive, ca. 1926. **88:** The Bettmann Archive, ca. 1900. **91:** Michael Weisbrat/Stock Boston. **92:** ©Jim Anderson/Stock Boston. **93:** ©Jean-Claude LeJeune/Stock Boston.

Cluster 4: 99: ©Cary Wolinsky/Stock Boston. **105:** AP/Wide World Photos. **106:** UPI/Bettmann Newsphotos; **107:** AP/Wide World Photos. **111:** ©Daniel S. Brody/Stock Boston. **117:** ©B. Barnes/Stock Boston. **119 (left):** ©Erich Hartmann/Magnum Photos. **119 (right):** ©Cary Wolinsky/Stock Boston. **124:** ©Peter Menzel/Stock Boston.

Illustrators

Gwen Connelly, Barbara Corey, Sharon Elzaurdia, Barbara Lanza, Susan C. Mills, John Walter, Jack Wallen